CHICKEN SOUP FOR THE SOUL™ AT WORK

101 Stories of Courage, Compassion and Creativity in the Workplace

Jack Canfield
Mark Victor Hansen
Maida Rogerson
Martin Rutte
Tim Clauss

Health Communications, Inc.
Deerfield Beach, Florida

We would like to acknowledge the following publishers and individuals for permission to reprint the following material. (Note: The stories that were penned anonymously, that are public domain or were written by Jack Canfield, Mark Victor Hansen, Maida Rogerson, Martin Rutte or Tim Clauss are not included in this listing.)

Jessie's Glove. Reprinted by permission of Rick Phillips. ©1996 Rick Phillips.

Climbing the Stairway to Heaven. Reprinted by permission of Joanna Slan. ©1996 Joanna Slan.

All in a Day's Work. Reprinted by permission of Naomi Rhode. ©1996 Naomi Rhode.

I Heard a Little Voice. Reprinted by permission of Anne Walton. ©1996 Anne Walton.

(Continued on page 326)

Library of Congress Cataloging-in-Publication Data

Chicken soup for the soul at work: 101 stories of courage, compassion, and creativity in the workplace / Jack Canfield . . . [et al.].
    p.   cm.
    ISBN 1-55874-424-X (trade paper)—ISBN 1-55874-430-4 (hardcover)
    1. Work—Moral and ethical aspects.   2. Interpersonal relations—Moral and ethical aspects.   3. Employees—Conduct of life.   4. Spiritual life.
    5. Inspiration—Anecdotes.   I. Canfield, Jack, date-   .
    HD4905.C448   1996   96-29381
    331.25—dc20   CIP

Publisher: Health Communications, Inc.
                 3201 S.W. 15th Street
                 Deerfield Beach, FL 33442-8190

Cover re-design by Andrea Perrine Brower

"Reading *Chicken Soup for the Soul at Work* is a poignant experience about ordinary men and women who touch other lives in an extraordinary way with acts of kindness, caring and love. It's a moving testament that responding to the Spirit is a wonderful way to transform our world and make it a better place."

Michael A. Stephen
chairman, Aetna International, Inc.

"As with the other *Chicken Soups, Chicken Soup for the Soul at Work* is an inspirational guide for being true to yourself under difficult circumstances, in trying times and on the job. A 'how-to' for being productive, effective and successful, while being human."

Jeffrey C. Reiss
chairman & CEO, CareerTrack

"It took a lot of talented minds to make this book as helpful and touching as it is. Great people produced some great reading!"

Og Mandino
speaker & author, *The Greatest Salesman in the World*

"This a wonderful, easy-to-read book that shows how little acts make big differences. It opens a new dimension in the workplace by giving people the freedom and permission to do what feels right inside."

Vikram Budhraja
senior vice president, Southern California Edison Co.

"Spirit, heart and ethics abound in these stories about work. They reflect the profound change that is taking place in the workplace."

Willis Harman
president, Institute of Noetic Sciences

"If you want to laugh, cry and feel good inside, read a few gems from *Chicken Soup for the Soul at Work.* Take it to work and make life a little richer for yourself and others. Great stories to share with your boss, coworkers and practically anyone!"

Michele Ann Marien, R.N., B.S.N.
emergency room nurse, Holy Cross Hospital

"If we need anything at work these days, it's more soul, and if *Chicken Soup for the Soul* is needed anywhere these days, it's at work. This book recognizes the spirit of work and its importance in our spiritual journey. It honors humanity and goodness in the workplace, and provides encouragement and wisdom to nurture the soul in an environment that is so often hard on the inner life. Take this book to work and put it to work in your life."

James A. Autry
author, *Love and Profit* and *Confessions of an Accidental Businessman*

"Work is about people. This book is about people. Stories of heart, insight and compassion—the true values of the workplace."

John Morgan
managing director, Peak Capital Corporation and former president, Labatt Brewing Company of Canada

"*Chicken Soup for the Soul at Work* is a sure-fire recipe for inspiring staff members at every level to follow their dreams, set their sights high, and never give up. Like its predecessor, *Chicken Soup for the Soul,* this new book is filled with heartwarming, inspirational stories that are sure to strike a responsive chord everywhere. It has the gift of making us all feel valued, treasured and important."

William J. Cirone
superintendent, Santa Barbara County Education Office

"When I'm feeling low, burned-out, tired and stressed, I know where to go. I open the book *Chicken Soup for the Soul at Work.*"

Danielle Kennedy
author, *Seven Figure Selling* and *Mother's in the Big League*

"They have outdone themselves again! This book will touch you where you work, and where you live; in your heart and soul; in your very bones. Required reading for every factory, farm and foundry."

Orvel Ray Wilson
coauthor, *Guerrilla Selling*

Where our work is, there let our joy be.
Tertullian

With love, we dedicate this
book to working souls everywhere for
your labors of love, service and purpose.
We deeply acknowledge your energy, creativity,
caring and commitment. May you, your
families and our world be blessed by
your unique contributions.

It's insulting the way Management treats us all like a bunch of children. But I *am* growing fond of story time.

Contents

1. LOVE AT WORK

2. ON CARING

3. THE POWER OF ACKNOWLEDGMENT

4. SERVICE: SETTING NEW STANDARDS

5. FOLLOW YOUR HEART

6. CREATIVITY AT WORK

7. OVERCOMING OBSTACLES

8. ON COURAGE

9. LESSONS & INSIGHTS

Acknowledgments

Chicken Soup for the Soul at Work has taken more than a year to write, compile and edit. It has been a true labor of cocreation for all of us. One of the greatest joys in creating this book has been working with people who gave this project not just their time and attention, but also their hearts and souls. We would like to thank the following people for their dedication and contributions, without which this book could not have been created:

Our families, who have given us love and support throughout this project, and who have been chicken soup for *our* souls!

Heather McNamara, for editing and preparing the final manuscript with such ease, grace and clarity. We deeply appreciate your patience, hard work and valuable suggestions. You are a joy to work with!

Patty Aubery, for her encouragement and inspiration, especially during the stress of final editing.

Nancy Mitchell, for her persistence and fortitude in obtaining the permissions for all the stories in this book.

Veronica Romero and Julie Knapp, for helping in Jack's office to make the day-to-day work run smoothly.

Rosalie Miller, who nourished us with her food and love in the final weeks of preparing the manuscript.

Trudy Klefsted at Office Works, for her overnight typing in the final stages of preparing the manuscript.

Sarah Ann Langston, who typed many of the stories under time pressure.

Valerie Santagto, for her photographic creativity and professionalism.

And our dear friend Douglas Blair for his love, encouragement and caring throughout our book-writing process.

A special thank you to the story authors for your inspiring contributions to this book. We hope their inclusion will expand your careers and further your self-expression in the world.

Our appreciation also to the hundreds of people who sent us stories, poems and quotes for possible inclusion in *Chicken Soup for the Soul at Work*. While we were not able to use everything that was sent in, we were deeply touched by your heartfelt intention to share yourselves and your stories with us and our readers.

We're also grateful to many of the contributors to previous *Chicken Soup for the Soul* books for their love of this project and their continued willingness to share their stories.

We also want to thank the people who read the first, very rough draft of over 160 stories, helped us make the final selections, and offered helpful comments on how to improve the book: Mavis Allred, Missy Alpern, Gina Armijo, Barbara Astrowsky, Shawn Berry, Douglas Blair, Rick Blake, Mike Blower, Leslie Boardman, Hal Bolton, Linda Bradley, Donna Burke, Mary Clark, Armond and Lorraine Clauss, Patricia Cole, Dr. Marlene M. Coleman, Amy Connolly, Sandford Daigle, Ron Delpier, Sander Feinberg, Susan and David Gardin, Fredelle Gudofsky, Douglas Hoover, Nick Kleto, Linda Masterson, Bob and Carolyn McClellan, Wally Michaels, Linda Naiman, Dave Potter, Ross Praskey, Amy Rogerson, John Scherer, Carol Schultz, Michael Shandler, Ellen Sloan, John St.

Augustine, Mary Tanton, Joan and Leith Thompson, and Roy Trueblood.

And the people who helped us out with stories at the last minute: Thea Alexander, Richard Barrett, Ken Blanchard, Charles Bower, Don Brown, Stephanie Clarke, Paul and Layne Cutright, Stan Dale, Chris Douglas, Burt Dubin, Nicholas Economou, Warren Farrell, Ann Feyerherm, John E. Foley, Kay Gilley, Scott Gross, Jennifer Hawthorne, Ron Hulnick, Karen Jorgensen, Kimberly Kirberger, Janet Larson, Steven Lawson, Diane Loomans, Dorothy Marcic, Judy Meyering and Diane Montgomery at CareerTrack, Jonathon Moyners, Bryan Murray, Richard Navarrette, Tim Piering, Morton Ritts, John Scherer, Ron Scoaslico, Marci Shimoff, Frank Siccone, Robert Siccone, Sue Smink at the Pryor Report, Pat Sullivan, Grant Sylvester, Marta Vago, Jonathan Wygant and Elsie F. Zala.

Peter Vegso and Gary Seidler at Health Communications, Inc., for believing in this book from the moment it was proposed, and for getting it into the hands of millions of readers. Thank you, Peter and Gary!

Christine Belleris, Matthew Diener and Mark Colucci, our editors at Health Communications, Inc., for their generous efforts in bringing this book to completion.

Arielle Ford and Kim Weiss, our publicists, who continue to get the word out about the *Chicken Soup* series.

Because of the enormity of this project, we may have left out the names of some people who helped us along the way. If so, we are sorry—please know that we really do appreciate each of you.

And finally, we are truly grateful to the living *Spirit* that inspires us. Through its presence in our lives, this work became play and a direct expression of our souls' true purpose.

Introduction

A successful businessman traveled to India to spend a month working in one of Mother Teresa's shelters. He longed to meet the tiny nun, but Mother Teresa was traveling, and it wasn't until the day before his departure that he received an audience. When he was finally in her presence, much to his surprise, he burst into tears. All the times when he'd been self-centered, busy or focused on his own gain flashed before his eyes, and he felt an enormous sadness that he had missed so many opportunities in his life to give of himself and his resources. Without a word, Mother Teresa walked over to where he was seated, put her hands on his shoulders and looked deeply into his eyes. "Don't you know," she said, "that God knows you are doing the best that you can."

Work is an integral part of our lives, filled with a wide variety of experiences. In writing this book, we received stories from teachers and engineers, carpenters and accountants, artists, managers, housekeepers, chiropractors—and workers from many other professions. Reading these stories, we have been deeply touched by the enormous heart, soul and spirit that people express through their work. Day after day, we all get up every morning, in many cases deal with a busy family, then go to work to spend 8, 10, even 12 hours making our contribution. This is commitment in action.

Sweeping and profound changes are occurring every day in the workplace, but we still long for our basic human needs to be met—meaningful relationships, creative fulfillment, and the knowledge that our work is valued and valuable.

There are definite signs that work is undergoing a renewal. This is reflected in our chapter headings, including The Power of Acknowledgment (Chapter 3)—discovering the life-affirming, positive energy of recognition; Service: Setting New Standards (Chapter 4)—exploring the richness of giving; and Follow Your Heart (Chapter 5)—emphasizing the value of intuitive knowing.

You can use these stories in many ways—as a good read, as fuel for reflection, as a respite you seek when you're down or you're up—but above all, please share them with your friends and co-workers. Let the stories lead you to discussion and sharing. If you're inspired, share your inspiration; if you're amused, share your laughter; if your heart is touched, reach out to another.

As we approach the new millennium, let's support each other in having the work we do be fulfilling, rewarding and a contribution to us all. As Thomas Aquinas said, "There is no joy in living without joy in work."

Reading these stories will remind you again, as it has reminded us, that when everything else is scraped away, we are working souls—loving, growing, always evolving—"doing the best that we can."

There is nothing better for a man than to eat and drink and tell himself that his labor is good.
Ecclesiastes 2:24

1

LOVE AT WORK

Work is love made visible.

Kahlil Gibran

Jessie's Glove

A kind and compassionate act is often its own reward.

William J. Bennett

I do a lot of management training each year for the Circle K Corporation, a national chain of convenience stores. Among the topics we address in our seminars is the retention of quality employees—a real challenge to managers when you consider the pay scale in the service industry. During these discussions, I ask the participants, "What has caused you to stay long enough to become a manager?" Some time back a new manager took the question and slowly, with her voice almost breaking, said, "It was a $19 baseball glove."

Cynthia told the group that she originally took a Circle K clerk job as an interim position while she looked for something better. On her second or third day behind the counter, she received a phone call from her nine-year-old son, Jessie. He needed a baseball glove for Little League. She explained that as a single mother, money was very tight, and her first check would have to go for paying bills. Perhaps she could buy his baseball glove with her second or third check.

When Cynthia arrived for work the next morning, Patricia, the store manager, asked her to come to the small room in back of the store that served as an office. Cynthia wondered if she had done something wrong or left some part of her job incomplete from the day before. She was concerned and confused.

Patricia handed her a box. "I overheard you talking to your son yesterday," she said, "and I know that it is hard to explain things to kids. This is a baseball glove for Jessie because he may not understand how important he is, even though you have to pay bills before you can buy gloves. You know we can't pay good people like you as much as we would like to; but we do care, and I want you to know you are important to us."

The thoughtfulness, empathy and love of this convenience store manager demonstrates vividly that people remember more how much an employer cares than how much the employer pays. An important lesson for the price of a Little League baseball glove.

Rick Phillips

Climbing the Stairway to Heaven

No one can deal with the hearts of men unless
he has the sympathy which is given by love.
Henry Ward Beecher

Throughout my career in sales, I've wondered about difficult customers. What makes them so mean? How can they be so unkind? How can a perfectly rational person suddenly lose all sense of human decency?

One day, I had an insight into their thinking. It happened while visiting my husband's music store. He was working with a customer and we were short-handed. So I did what every good wife would do: I tried to wait on customers.

"I'm looking for music," said a gnarled man, a soiled John Deere cap pulled down tightly over his thinning gray hair. "The name of the song is . . ." and he uncrumpled a grimy sheet of mimeographed paper from his jeans pocket, "'Stairway to Heaven.' Do you have it?"

I stepped to the wall displays of sheet music and scanned for the name. On a good day, the music filled slots in alphabetical order. On this day, the alphabet skipped around. I searched for several minutes, conscious of his growing restlessness.

"No, I'm sorry but it doesn't look like it's here."

His back arched and his watery blue eyes narrowed. Almost imperceptibly, his wife touched his sleeve as if to draw him back. His narrow mouth twisted in anger.

"Well, ain't that just grand. You call yourself a music store? What kind of a store doesn't have music like that? All the kids know that song!" he spluttered.

"Yes, but we don't carry every piece of music ever . . ."

"Oh, easy for you! Easy to give excuses!" Now his wife was pawing at his sleeve, murmuring, trying to calm him the way a groom talks to a horse gone wild.

He leaned in to me, pointing a knotty finger at my face. "I guess you wouldn't understand, would you? You don't care about my boy dying! About him smashing up his Camaro into that old tree. About them playing his favorite song at his funeral, and he's dead! He's gone! Only 18 and he's gone!"

The paper he waved at me came into focus. It was the program for a memorial service.

"I guess you wouldn't understand," he mumbled. He bent his head. His wife put her arm around him and stood quietly by his side.

"I can't understand your loss," I said quietly, "but we buried my four-year-old nephew last month, and I know how bad that hurts."

He looked up at me. The anger slid from his face, and he sighed. "It's a shame, ain't it? A dirty shame." We stood in silence for a long moment. Then he fished around in his back pocket and pulled out a worn billfold. "Would you like to see a picture of our boy?"

Joanna Slan

"Whatever You Need"

That which cometh from the heart goes to the heart.

Jeremiah Burroughs

I was working as a consultant in a beer company, helping the president and senior vice-presidents formulate and implement their new strategic vision. It was an enormous challenge.

At the same time, my mother was in the final stages of cancer.

I worked during the day and drove 40 miles home to be with her every night. It was tiring and stressful, but it was what I wanted to do. My commitment was to continue to do excellent consulting during the day, even though my evenings were very hard. I didn't want to bother the president with my situation, yet I felt someone at the company needed to know what was going on. So I told the vice-president of Human Resources, asking him not to share the information with anyone.

A few days later, the president called me into his office.

I figured he wanted to talk to me about one of the many issues we were working on. When I entered, he asked me to sit down. He faced me from across his large desk, looked me in the eye and said, "I hear your mother is very ill."

I was totally caught by surprise and burst into tears. He just looked at me, let my crying subside, and then gently said a sentence I will never forget: "Whatever you need."

That was it. His understanding and his willingness to both let me be in my pain and to offer me everything were qualities of compassion that I carry with me to this day.

Martin Rutte

What you need, Mr. Terwilliger, is a bit of human caring; a gentle, reassuring touch; a warm smile that shows concern—all of which, I'm afraid, were not part of my medical training.

Reprinted with permission from Harley Schwadron.

All in a Day's Work

If I can ease one life the aching,
or cool one pain,
or help one fainting robin
unto his nest again,
I shall not live in vain.

Emily Dickinson

He was admitted to emergency receiving and placed on the cardiac floor. Long hair, unshaven, dirty, dangerously obese, with a black motorcycle jacket tossed on the bottom shelf of the stretcher, he was an outsider to this sterile world of shining terrazzo floors, efficient uniformed professionals, and strict infection control procedures. Definitely an untouchable.

The nurses at the station looked wide-eyed as this mound of humanity was wheeled by, each glancing nervously at Bonnie, the head nurse. "Let this one not be mine to admit, bathe and tend to . . ." was their pleading, unspoken message.

One of the true marks of a leader, a consummate

professional, is to do the unthinkable. To tackle the impossible. To touch the untouchable. It was Bonnie who said, "I want this patient myself." Highly unusual for a head nurse—unconventional—but the stuff out of which human spirits thrive, heal and soar.

As she donned her latex gloves and proceeded to bathe this huge, very unclean man, her heart almost broke. Where was his family? Who was his mother? What was he like as a little boy? She hummed quietly as she worked. It seemed to ease the fear and embarrassment she knew he must be feeling.

And then on a whim she said, "We don't have time for back rubs much in hospitals these days, but I bet one would really feel good. And it would help you relax your muscles and start to heal. That is what this place is all about . . . a place to heal."

The thick, scaly, ruddy skin told a story of an abusive lifestyle: probably lots of addictive behavior with food, alcohol and drugs. As she rubbed those taut muscles, she hummed and prayed. Prayed for the soul of a little boy grown up, rejected by life's rudeness and striving for acceptance in a hard, hostile world.

The finale was warmed lotion and baby powder. Almost laughable—such a contrast to this huge, foreign surface. As he rolled over onto his back, tears ran down his cheeks and his chin trembled. With amazingly beautiful brown eyes, he smiled and said in a quivering voice, "No one has touched me for years. Thank you. I am healing."

Naomi Rhode

I Heard a Little Voice

It takes great courage to faithfully follow what we know to be true.

Sara E. Anderson

I was working with a young man who was in his early 30s and fairly close to death. His parents had come from out of town and were spending as much time as possible with him at the hospital. They had been with him for many hours and finally took a break to go out for dinner. While they were out, their son died. The parents were devastated, the man's mother in particular; not only had her son died, but he had died during her absence. She was obviously distressed and frequently rested her head on her son's chest and cried.

As I was standing with her, I distinctly heard a little voice in my head say, *Suggest that she get up on the bed and hold him.* My mind whizzed. *How could I make such a suggestion? What if someone saw? What would people think?* I tried to ignore the voice, hoping it would go away. Not so. Seconds later, the voice said in a louder, more insistent tone, *She needs to get up on the bed and hold him!*

"Would you like to get up on the bed and hold him?" I heard myself ask. She all but leapt onto it. I remained with her while she held her son, stroked his face, talked with him and sang to him. Those moments with this mother and her son were some of the most exquisite moments of my life. I felt blessed that I was able to be with her while she said good-bye to her child.

Anne Walton

The Christmas Man

*When we quit thinking primarily about our-
selves and our own self-preservation, we undergo
a truly heroic transformation of consciousness.*

Joseph Campbell

Last Christmas was a very difficult time for me. My
family and all of my close friends were back home in
Florida, and I was all alone in a rather cold California. I
was working too many hours and became very sick.

I was working a double shift at the Southwest Airlines
ticket counter, it was about 9:00 P.M. on Christmas Eve, and
I was feeling really miserable inside. There were a few of us
working and very few customers waiting to be helped.
When it was time for me to call the next person to the
counter, I looked out to see the sweetest-looking old man
standing with a cane. He walked very slowly over to the
counter and in the faintest voice told me that he had to go
to New Orleans. I tried to explain to him that there were no
more flights that night and that he would have to go in the
morning. He looked so confused and very worried. I tried to

find out more information by asking if he had a reservation or if he remembered when he was supposed to travel, but he seemed to become more confused with each question. He just kept saying, "She said I have to go to New Orleans."

After much time, I was able to at least find out that this old man was dropped off at the curb on Christmas Eve by his sister-in-law and told to go to New Orleans, where he had family. She had given him some cash and told him just to go inside and buy a ticket. When I asked if he could come back tomorrow, he said that she was gone and that he had no place to stay. He then said he would wait at the airport until tomorrow. Naturally, I felt a little ashamed. Here I was feeling very sorry for myself about being alone on Christmas, when this angel named Clarence MacDonald was sent to me to remind me of what being alone really meant. It broke my heart.

Immediately, I told him we would get it all straightened out, and our Customer Service agent helped to book him a seat for the earliest flight the next morning. We gave him the senior citizens' fare, which gave him some extra money for traveling. About this time he started to look very tired, and when I stepped around the counter to ask him if he was all right, I saw that his leg was wrapped in a bandage. He had been standing on it that whole time, holding a plastic bag full of clothes.

I called for a wheelchair. When the wheelchair came, we all stepped around to help him in, and I noticed a small amount of blood on his bandage. I asked how he hurt his leg, and he said that he had just had bypass surgery and an artery was taken from his leg. *Can you imagine?* This man had had heart surgery, and then shortly afterward, was dropped off at the curb to buy a ticket with no reservation to fly to New Orleans, alone!

I never really had a situation like this, and I wasn't sure what I could do. I went back to ask my supervisors if we could find a place for him to stay. They both said yes, and they obtained a hotel voucher for Mr. MacDonald for one night and a meal ticket for dinner and breakfast. When I came back out, we got his plastic bag of clothes and cane together and gave the porter a tip to take him downstairs to wait for the airport shuttle. I bent down to explain the hotel, food and itinerary again to Mr. MacDonald, and then patted him on the arm and told him everything would be just fine.

As he left he said, "Thank you," bent his head and started to cry. I cried too. When I went back to thank my supervisor, she just smiled and said, "I love stories like that. He is your Christmas Man."

Rachel Dyer Montross

His Life's Work

Let the beauty of what you love be what you do.

Rumi

When his wife died, the baby was two. They had six other children—three boys and three girls, ranging in age from 4 to 16.

A few days after he became a widower, the man's parents and his deceased wife's parents came to visit.

"We've been talking," they said, "about how to make this work. There's no way you can take care of all these children and work to make a living. So, we've arranged for each child to be placed with a different uncle and aunt. We're making sure that all of your children will be living right here in the neighborhood, so you can see them anytime . . ."

"You have no idea how much I appreciate your thoughtfulness," the man responded. "But I want you to know," he smiled and continued, "if the children should interfere with my work, or if we should need any help, we'll let you know."

Over the next few weeks the man worked with his children, assigning them chores and giving them responsibilities. The two older girls, aged 12 and 10, began to cook and do the laundry and household chores. The two older boys, 16 and 14, helped their father with his farming.

But then another blow. The man developed arthritis. His hands swelled, and he was unable to grip the handles of his farm tools. The children shouldered their loads well, but the man could see that he would not be able to continue in this vein. He sold his farming equipment, moved the family to a small town and opened a small business.

The family was welcomed into the new neighborhood. The man's business flourished. He derived pleasure from seeing people and serving them. Word of his pleasant personality and excellent customer service began to spread. People came from far and wide to do business with him. And the children helped both at home and at work. Their father's pleasure in his work brought satisfaction to them, and he drew pleasure from their successes.

The children grew up and got married. Five of the seven went off to college, most after they were married. Each one paid his or her own way. The children's collegiate successes were a source of pride to the father. He had stopped at the sixth grade.

Then came grandchildren. No one enjoyed grandchildren more than this man. As they became toddlers, he invited them to his workplace and his small home. They brought each other great joy.

Finally, the youngest daughter—the baby, who had been two years old at her mother's death—got married.

And the man, his life's work completed, died.

This man's work had been the lonely but joyful task of raising his family. This man was my father. I was the 16-year-old, the oldest of seven.

Wyverne Flatt

For the Love of My Father

*Love conquers all things; let us too surrender
to love.*

Virgil

Over the years, I never thought of my father as being
very emotional, and he never was, at least not in front of
me. Even though he was 68 years old and only five-foot-
nine, while I was six feet and 260 pounds, he seemed huge
to me. I always saw him as being that staunch disciplinar-
ian who rarely cracked a smile. My father never told me
he loved me when I was a child, and I never held it against
him. I think that all I really wanted was for my dad to be
proud of me. In my youth, Mom always showered me
with "I love you's" every day. So I really never thought
about not hearing it from my dad. I guess deep down I
knew that he loved me, he just never said it. Come to
think of it, I don't think I ever told him that I loved him,
either. I never really thought about it much until I faced
the reality of death.

On November 9th, 1990, I received word that my National Guard unit was being activated for Operation Desert Shield. We would convoy to Fort Ben Harrison, Indiana, and then directly to Saudi Arabia. I had been in the Guard for 10 years and never dreamed that we would be activated for a war, even though I knew it was what we trained for. I went to my father and gave him the news. I could sense he was uneasy about me going. We never discussed it much more, and eight days later I was gone.

I have several close relatives who have been in the military during war time. My father and uncle were in World War II, and two brothers and a sister served in Vietnam. While I was extremely uneasy about leaving my family to serve my country in a war zone, I knew it was what I had to do. I prayed that this would make my father proud of me. My father is very involved in the Veterans of Foreign Wars organization and has always been for a strong military. I was not eligible to join the Veterans of Foreign Wars because I had not been in a war zone—a fact that always made me feel like I didn't measure up in my father's eyes. But now here I was, his youngest son, being shipped off to a foreign land 9,000 miles away, to fight a war in a country we had barely heard of before.

On November 17, 1990, our convoy of military vehicles rolled out of rural Greenville, Michigan. The streets were filled with families and well-wishers to see us off. As we approached the edge of town, I looked out the window of my truck and saw my wife, Kim, my children, and Mom and Dad. They were all waving and crying, except for my father. He just stood there, almost like a stone statue. He looked incredibly old at that moment. I don't know why, he just did.

I was gone for that Thanksgiving and missed our family's dinner. There was always a crowd, with two of my sisters, their husbands and children, plus my wife and our family. It disturbed me greatly that I couldn't be there. A few days after Thanksgiving I was able to call my wife, and she told me something that has made me look at my father in a different way ever since.

My wife knew how my father was about his emotions, and I could hear her voice quaver as she spoke to me. She told me that my father recited his usual Thanksgiving prayer. But this time he added one last sentence. As his voice started to crack and a tear ran down his cheek, he said, "Dear Lord, please watch over and guide my son, Rick, with your hand in his time of need as he serves his country, and bring him home to us safely." At that point he burst into tears. I had never seen my father cry, and when I heard this, I couldn't help but start to cry myself. My wife asked me what was wrong. After regaining my composure, I said, "I guess my father really does love me."

Eight months later, when I returned home from the war, I ran over and hugged my wife and children in a flurry of tears. When I came to my father, I embraced him and gave him a huge hug. He whispered in my ear, "I'm very proud of you, Son, and I love you." I looked that man, my dad, straight in the eyes as I held his head between my hands and I said, "I love you too, Dad," and we embraced again. And then together, both of us cried.

Ever since that day, my relationship with my father has never been the same. We have had many deep conversations. I learned that he's always been proud of me, and he's not afraid to say "I love you" anymore. Neither am I. I'm just sorry it took 29 years and a war to find it out.

Rick Halvorsen

2

ON CARING

The power of love and caring can change the world.

James Autry

A Lesson from My Father

You make a living by what you get, but you make a life by what you give.

Anonymous

We come by business naturally in our family. Each of the seven children in our family worked in our father's store, "Our Own Hardware-Furniture Store," in Mott, North Dakota, a small town on the prairies. We started working by doing odd jobs like dusting, arranging shelves and wrapping, and later graduated to serving customers. As we worked and watched, we learned that work was about more than survival and making a sale.

One lesson stands out in my mind. It was shortly before Christmas. I was in the eighth grade and was working evenings, straightening the toy section. A little boy, five or six years old, came in. He was wearing a brown tattered coat with dirty worn cuffs. His hair was straggly, except for a cowlick that stood straight up from the crown of his head. His shoes were scuffed and his one shoelace was torn. The little boy looked poor to me—too poor to afford to buy anything. He looked around the toy section, picked up this item and that, and carefully put them back in their place.

Dad came down the stairs and walked over to the boy. His steel blue eyes smiled and the dimple in his cheek stood out as he asked the boy what he could do for him. The boy said he was looking for a Christmas present to buy his brother. I was impressed that Dad treated him with the same respect as any adult. Dad told him to take his time and look around. He did.

After about 20 minutes, the little boy carefully picked up a toy plane, walked up to my dad and said, "How much for this, Mister?"

"How much you got?" Dad asked.

The little boy held out his hand and opened it. His hand was creased with wet lines of dirt from clutching his money. In his hand lay two dimes, a nickel and two pennies—27 cents. The price on the toy plane he'd picked out was $3.98.

"That'll just about do it," Dad said as he closed the sale. Dad's reply still rings in my ears. I thought about what I'd seen as I wrapped the present. When the little boy walked out of the store, I didn't notice the dirty, worn coat, the straggly hair, or the single torn shoelace. What I saw was a radiant child with a treasure.

LaVonn Steiner

Bringing Your Heart to Work

You can handle people more successfully by enlisting their feelings than by convincing their reason.

Paul P. Parker

A corporate client subcontracted with me to train the major telemarketing firm she worked for. While training the telemarketing staff in sales, I noticed agitation among them. They were learning a new sales technology that combines trust, integrity and collaboration in supporting a prospect's buying decisions. They worked hard and were excited about learning, but it was obvious they were holding back their full commitment. By the end of the first day, I knew I couldn't continue without a full under-standing of what was going on with the team.

"Is there a problem with you learning this technology?" I asked. They sat silently. I waited for an answer. Finally, someone spoke.

"It would be great if we could really use this stuff. I mean, I can see where it would really work, and I wouldn't have to feel like I'm being so abusive to the people I'm calling. But I don't really think the company will let us use it. They don't care about people. They treat us like sub-humans, use abusive selling tactics for prospects and only care about the bottom line. If they found out we were using this type of approach they'd put a stop to it."

I told the group I'd think about the problem and made a commitment to assist them in finding a way to integrate the new skills. They seemed to be happy to try, but unconvinced that I could make a difference.

Following the program, I went to the telephone bank where the salespeople worked and watched while the company's senior vice-president came over to speak with one of the representatives. He interrupted her in the middle of a conversation. He then walked over to another person who was on a sales call and asked him why he had a personal photo on his desk, since none were allowed. At the desk where I was sitting was a memo from the same man, telling people they had to wear suits the following day and keep their suit jackets on between 11:00 A.M. and noon because prospective clients would be coming through the office.

I waited until the senior vice-president went back to his office and knocked on his door. Since I teach collabora-tion, I decided to assume we were in a win-win situation. He smiled and invited me to speak. "I've got a problem that I'm hoping you can solve. I've been hired to teach this new sales technology that really supports trust and collaboration. However, the participants are afraid to bring it back to their desks."

He was a big man and an ex-Marine. He sat way back in his chair and rocked, smiling at me over a well-fed stomach. He replied, "If it makes money, why should they be afraid?"

I took a good look at the man. He seemed gentle, although his actions didn't indicate that. "Do you mind if

I ask you a really personal question that may have nothing to do with anything?" I asked. His smile broadened
and he nodded as he rocked. I felt his acceptance of me.

"How do you function at work each day when you
leave your heart at home?"

The man continued to rock gently, never changing his
expression. I watched while his eyes narrowed. He
responded, "What else do you know about me?"

"It's confusing for me," I ventured. "You seem to be a
gentle person, yet your actions don't seem to take people
into account. You're putting task before relationship, but
somehow I think you know the difference."

He looked at his watch and asked, "Are you free for dinner? Come on, it's on me."

Our dinner lasted three hours. He graphically recounted
his Vietnam experiences as an officer who had to do bad
things to good people. He cried, I cried. His shame had kept
him silent, and he had never discussed the experiences
with anyone before. He spent his life believing that his
goodness could hurt people, so he decided years before not
to let his heart get in the way of his job. It was a pain he carried daily. His sharing gave me the permission to talk about
one of my own pains in my life that I rarely shared.
Together we sat with cold food, warm beers and tears.

The next morning he called me into his office. "Could
you sit with me while I do something?" he asked. Then he
called in the woman who had hired me, and apologized
for not supporting her and for being disrespectful to her
in front of others. She was shocked and grateful. He then
turned to me and asked, "Is there anything else you think
I should do?"

I thought for a moment and replied, "You may want to
consider apologizing to the entire team."

Without hesitation, he picked up the phone and asked
his secretary to call in the team for a quick meeting. There,

he apologized to the client in front of the team, apologized to the team for being disrespectful to them, and offered to make whatever changes they needed, so that they would want to come in to work each day. He also wanted to learn my technology and offer it to his entire sales staff.

That was the first of several meetings between the senior vice-president, my client and the team. People who were looking for new jobs stopped looking. People began to trust that being at work wouldn't be harmful and might even be fun. The team supported the new collaborative sales approach. The senior vice-president began to use his new skills with other teams. And I got a new friend.

Sharon Drew Morgen

A Pebble in the Water

We are confronted with insurmountable opportunities.

Walt Kelly, "Pogo"

The events leading up to the proudest moment in my 28-year teaching career began on Monday, December 9, 1990. Our troops were engaged in Desert Storm in Saudi Arabia. I was in an after-school faculty meeting in the high school cafeteria. The computer coordinator told us about Project Desert Shield, created by former Chicago Bears football great, Walter Payton.

She explained that he had chartered a plane for Sunday to fly to the Persian Gulf to personally deliver gifts and donated items from the Chicago metropolitan area. We were asked to invite our students to sign Christmas cards, and to write pen pal letters to cheer up our soldiers during the holidays.

As I was driving to school that Tuesday, I remembered spending Christmas in the Philippine Islands when I was in the Peace Corps in the 1960s. I had received cookies from home. What a difference they made! I had felt loved and cared for. I started thinking that if each student contributed 50 cents, we would have $60 to buy cookies to send on the plane on Sunday.

When I asked each of my five classes that Tuesday about contributing 50 cents, I got total support. As the day progressed and word spread about our cookie project, the National Honor Society volunteered to contribute paperbacks. Then the work program coordinator said her class would fill up Christmas stockings with candy.

On Wednesday morning, I went to the main office and told the principal's secretary about my students raising money for cookies, and what the other classes were doing. I asked her if the administration would make a donation. The principal agreed. I was so delighted that I then asked her if she would call the district office and see if the central administration would also contribute. They, too, agreed to support our project.

When I gave my class a running total of what we had collected, we decided that we were going to have over $150 to spend, so we could purchase more than cookies. We compiled a list of items that family members were encouraged to send overseas, and three students from each class volunteered to form a shopping committee.

On Thursday, I went to the faculty lounge for lunch and enthusiastically shared the news of the school's involvement in Project Desert Shield. One listener said that sand insects were getting into packages sent overseas and suggested I call a popcorn company to see if it would donate empty metal containers.

In addition to empty containers, the popcorn company offered to donate several cases of popcorn. When I gave my daily report to the classes and told them the response from the popcorn company, my students started brainstorming about other ways they could help through their parents' workplaces.

By the end of the school day on Thursday, we had collected $260. Armed with an official letter telling about the school's involvement in Project Desert Shield, our shopping committee members left to make their purchases.

When I got to my classroom on Friday morning, I was surprised to find the custodians unloading flats of boxes. The 15 committee members came in, one by one, with their purchases. They were very excited. They told me that they had difficulty paying for anything because the merchants wanted to make donations. We were so overwhelmed with boxes and cases, we couldn't fit them all into the school van. The principal had to call central administration and request a truck. We filled that truck with over $2,000 in products. Then we all gathered at the back of the truck for a picture with a banner that read, "Elk Grove Cares . . . Merry Christmas!"

I went back to my empty classroom, where a few hours before the room had been filled with animated and purposeful students. I thought how fulfilling this project had been and how much support and encouragement I had received. I remember sitting there in the silence, thinking, *Okay, God, I get it. I know now why I'm in the classroom.*

The following Monday, I asked each of my students to write a paragraph on Project Desert Shield. Some wrote that they would get involved in the community when they grew up. A few mentioned how one person can make a difference, and one said it was like the ripples that form when you throw a pebble in the water.

But the response that touched me the most was the one by the student who wrote, "Mrs. O'Brien, I was ready to kill myself this week. Then I got on the committee and saw I was accepted by the others, and . . . thank you."

Sally K. O'Brien

I Just Can't Believe It

*Our lives will always be full if our hearts are
always giving.*

Anonymous

After 30 years of service with American Airlines, I
retired after my 50th birthday. At this point, I finally
began what God had intended for me to do with the last
half of my life: to inspire, to motivate and to create *special
moments.*

In June of 1995, I stopped at the local service station
where I regularly get my gas and occasionally buy a lottery ticket. Millie was on duty. She is a kind and loving
soul who always has a smile on her face and a kind word
for everyone. On that evening, we joked and laughed as
we had so many times in the past. I teased her by saying that I would give her $1,000 if I won the $10-million
lottery. Millie said that if I won I'd better take her to
Paris for lunch, and she didn't mean Paris, Texas. We
both got a big "Texas kick" out of that. As I drove off, I
thought how interesting it was that for me, "lottery"

equaled $10 million, while for Millie, it meant lunch in Paris. Millie didn't know of my connection with the airlines.

Around the 21st of December, I was once again at the service station. Millie was on duty. I handed her a Christmas card and asked that she open it and read it as I stood there. Millie opened the card and started reading:

> *Dear Millie,*
>
> *On June 17, 1995, you sold me this lottery ticket (enclosed). Well, I didn't win the $10 million or the lottery, but you did. Pick your date in 1996, pack your bags, and get your passport ready for your luncheon trip to Paris. This is my gift to you for going out of your way to make everyone you come into contact with feel special. Thank you. God bless you, and have a Mary's Merry Christmas.*

Millie could not contain herself. She was literally thrashing around in the little cubicle. I could hardly contain myself, either. At that moment, at a soul level, I understood what it meant to create special moments for the people in our lives.

Over the past few weeks, I've seen Millie several times. Each time I enter the service station, her face lights up as she reaches across the half-opened door to hug my neck and kiss my face. She speaks of how she still "just can't believe it," how she phoned her mom, told her boss, and on and on. But what touched me the most was when Millie told me, "Mary Ann, it says in my will that if I died before I got that lunch, my instructions were to have my ashes sprinkled over Paris."

Mary Ann Dockins

Angel on a Doorstep

I can have peace of mind only when I forgive rather than judge.

Gerald Jampolsky

When Ben delivered milk to my cousin's home that morning, he wasn't his usual sunny self. The slight, middle-aged man seemed in no mood for talking.

It was late November 1962, and as a newcomer to Lawndale, California, I was delighted that milkmen still brought bottles of milk to doorsteps. In the weeks that my husband, kids and I had been staying with my cousin while house-hunting, I had come to enjoy Ben's jovial repartee.

Today, however, he was the epitome of gloom as he dropped off his wares from his wire carrier. It took slow, careful questioning to extract the story from him. With some embarrassment, he told me two customers had left town without paying their bills, and he would have to cover the losses. One of the debtors owed only $10, but the other was $79 in arrears and had left no forwarding address. Ben was distraught at his stupidity for allowing this bill to grow so large.

"She was a pretty woman," he said, "with six children and another on the way. She was always saying, 'I'm going to pay you soon, when my husband gets a second job.' I believed her. What a fool I was! I thought I was doing a good thing, but I've learned my lesson. I've been had!"

All I could say was, "I'm so sorry."

The next time I saw him, his anger seemed worse. He bristled as he talked about the messy young kids who had drunk up all his milk. The charming family had turned into a parcel of brats.

I repeated my condolences and let the matter rest. But when Ben left, I found myself caught up in his problem and longed to help. Worried that this incident would sour a warm person, I mulled over what to do. Then, remembering that Christmas was coming, I thought of what my grandmother used to say: "When someone has taken from you, give it to them, and then you can never be robbed."

The next time Ben delivered milk, I told him I had a way to make him feel better about the $79.

"Nothing will do that," he said, "but tell me anyway."

"*Give* the woman the milk. Make it a Christmas present to the kids who needed it."

"Are you kidding?" he replied. "I don't even get my wife a Christmas gift that expensive."

"The Bible says, 'I was a stranger and you took me in.' You just took her in with all her little children."

"Don't you mean she took *me* in? The trouble with you is, it wasn't *your* $79."

I let the subject drop, but I still believed in my suggestion.

We'd joke about it when he'd come. "Have you given her the milk yet?" I'd ask.

"No," he'd snap back, "but I'm thinking of giving my wife a $79 present, unless another pretty mother starts playing on my sympathies."

Every time I'd ask the question, he seemed to lighten up a bit more.

Then six days before Christmas, it happened. He arrived with a tremendous smile and a glint in his eyes. "I did it! I gave her the milk as a Christmas present. It wasn't easy, but what did I have to lose? It was gone, wasn't it?"

"Yes," I said, rejoicing with him, "but you've got to really mean it in your heart."

"I know," he said. "I do. And I really feel better. That's why I have this good feeling about Christmas. Those kids had lots of milk on their cereal just because of me."

The holidays came and went. On a sunny January morning two weeks later, Ben almost ran up the walk. "Wait till you hear this," he said, grinning.

He explained he had been on a different route, covering for another milkman. He heard his name being called, looked over his shoulder and saw a woman running down the street, waving money. He recognized her immediately—the pretty woman with all the kids, the one who hadn't paid her bill. She was carrying an infant in a tiny blanket.

"Ben, wait a minute!" she shouted. "I've got money for you."

Ben stopped the truck and got out.

"I'm so sorry," she said. "I really have been meaning to pay you." She explained that her husband had come home one night and announced he'd found a cheaper apartment. He'd also started a night job. With all that had happened, she'd forgotten to leave a forwarding address. "But I've been saving," she said. "Here's $20 toward the bill."

"That's all right," Ben replied. "It's been paid."

"Paid!" she exclaimed. "What do you mean? Who paid it?"

"I did."

She looked at him as if he were the Angel Gabriel and started to cry.

"Well," I asked, when Ben had finished recounting the story, "what did you do?"

"I didn't know what to do, so I put an arm around her. Before I knew what was happening, I started to cry, and I didn't have the foggiest idea what I was crying about. Then I thought of all those kids having milk on their cereal, and you know what? I was really glad you talked me into this."

"You didn't take the $20?"

"Heck no," he replied indignantly. "I gave her the milk as a Christmas present, didn't I?"

Shirley Bachelder

Santa Comes to Joan

Friendships multiply joys and divide grief.

Thomas Fuller

Every office has a Joan, or should have. She's the one everyone looks to when the workload gets too heavy. She's the one with the good story and the ready laugh. For our Christmas party, she's the one who transforms our sterile corporate conference room, Christmas after Christmas, with linen tablecloths, miniature Christmas trees with tiny white lights, real teacups, teapots and plates she had brought from home.

Joan is also a breast cancer survivor who was diagnosed with lung cancer early this year. It has been a very difficult time for her, facing her own mortality again, and suffering from a vision problem that not only has added further complications to her health and well-being, but has also caused her to miss many days of work. This has added financial stress to her medical concerns. So this year, instead of drawing names and giving each other gifts at Christmas, we put our dollars together for Joan.

At the Christmas party, we presented her with a series of gift certificates.

Joan's vision problem had been a daily battle. At times, taking her turn to relieve the receptionist at the switchboard, Joan couldn't see the numbers well enough to transfer callers to the right extension. Her doctor had prescribed new glasses, but she hadn't filled the prescription because she didn't have the money. The first gift certificate was for a new pair of eyeglasses.

We live in Minnesota, where the winters are extremely cold and heating bills can be formidable. Joan didn't know what she was going to do this year. The next certificate was for payment toward her gas bill.

Because she is a cancer patient, Joan has been encouraged to include more fresh fruits and vegetables in her diet. We decided to help her do what's best for her body with a grocery certificate.

And finally, we gave her a certificate to a local department store, all for her.

Joan accepted our gifts with a gracious spirit and thanked us for giving her courage on the really bad days. Then she told us that when she was six or seven, the kids at school told her there was no Santa Claus. That year, she asked for things she knew her parents couldn't afford, just to test dear old Santa. Her mother, determined that at least for one more year Joan would believe, managed to get everything on Joan's list.

This year, Joan told us, felt like that long-ago Christmas. She could now believe once again that dreams really did come true. It was our best Christmas party ever.

Angela Barnett

The Arc Angels

It is better to give and receive.

Bernard Gunther

Several years ago, Iris Arc Crystal, a company I co-founded with Francesca Patruno, experienced a lull in business. We had recently hired several new employees and hoped that the slowdown was only temporary. However, in the meantime, we had work enough for only four days of the week. So, instead of letting 20 percent of our work force go or sending them home one day per week, we decided that we would keep everyone on the payroll for the entire week, working from Monday through Thursday, and taking Fridays to do service projects in our hometown of Santa Barbara.

I remember phoning several service agencies to find out what was needed in the community. We divided up into three groups and showed up where the agencies said they most needed us. The first week, the group I was involved with went to a very old Ukrainian gentleman's home to do a total cleanup of his house and garden.

When we arrived, an elderly woman greeted us at the door. We thought she was the wife, but it turned out she was the daughter. She was 75, and her father was 97! She told us what we needed to do, and we proceeded to clean the house from floor to ceiling and clean up the yard as well. It is amazing how much work a group can get done when everyone is working together and being of service to someone who really needs the help. That gentleman's house went from dirt and dinginess to a sparkling clean palace by the time we finished at the end of the day.

The thing I most remember about that day, however, was not the great cleaning job that we did, but something altogether different. When we first walked into the house, I noticed the wonderful pen-and-ink drawings that adorned the walls in all the rooms of the house. I asked the daughter who had done them. She said that her father had, and that he hadn't taken up art until he was 80 years old! I was dumbfounded; these drawings were works of art that could have easily been hanging in a museum. At the time, I was in my early 30s and wanted to do something that would utilize my creative and artistic capabilities more than being the president of a giftware company would allow. I had been feeling that it would be too difficult to make a change at this "advanced" stage of my life. Boy, did my limited belief system get expanded that afternoon!

We continued to do service projects around town for several more weeks, including completely painting someone's home and setting up a large bleacher for a horseback riding academy for physically challenged children. We had a lot of fun and did a lot of good. Somehow we ended up with the nickname The Arc Angels. In addition to the good feelings that came from helping out others, the good feelings we shared as employees of a company that cared for both its employees and the community went a long way toward creating a work atmosphere that was a joy to be part of.

Jonathan Wygant

The Break I Got from Prison

We know what we are, but know not what we may be.

William Shakespeare

A murderer tends my garden. An executive in my company has a prison record for robbery. One of the best foremen in my factory was once wanted by the police in eight states. Hundreds of my employees—and my friends—could tell you anything you want to know about life in a penitentiary. I could tell you myself. I am an ex-convict.

Prison marks a man. He goes there to pay the debt for the crime he committed against society, but when his term ends, society rarely gives him a paid-in-full receipt. Nobody wants him. The only route open for him leads back to crime. I know; it almost happened to me.

At 17, I decided I wanted to see the world. I had already seen quite a lot of it. My family owned a saloon and, because it kept them so busy, I had my time to myself. I earned spending money shining shoes, selling newspapers, delivering groceries and doing odd jobs around the tavern.

I quit the Denny Hill High School and ran away from my Seattle home. The years rushed by. I became a sailor, I drove an Arctic dog team; I panned for gold in Alaska. When Pancho Villa formed his army in Mexico, I joined him.

They were hectic years—rough years, and inescapably, they often took me to the fringe of the underworld. But just the fringe. I soon learned, however, that even this can be too close.

In 1919, I was arrested in Denver for possessing narcotics. I'd never had anything to do with narcotics. But nobody believed me; my vagabond life was too flavored with fringe adventures to defend my innocence. Convicted of the charge, I was sent to Leavenworth. And there, I got the one thing prisoners rarely get—a break.

My break came from my cellmate, Herbert Huse Bigelow, who was serving a term for income tax evasion. Both of us worked in the electric shop, and I eventually became the chief electrician. I decided that I wouldn't let the fact that I was unjustly imprisoned embitter me, and to keep myself occupied, I volunteered for extra work.

Herbert Bigelow worked with me on several of the projects. We became good friends. He was released ahead of me, and when he left, he offered me a job at the St. Paul company of which he was president. I considered this offer a good break. I made up my mind then that someday I'd give another convict a break.

In 1924, I went to work for Herbert Bigelow. Working hard, I received regular promotions. Nine years later I was general manager of the firm. When Herbert Bigelow died in 1933, I was chosen president of the company.

But I didn't wait until then to fulfill the promise I had made to myself. As soon as I was in a position to have a voice in employment matters, I got in touch with men I knew in prison and offered them jobs.

In time, that promise to myself became company policy, as we grew from 728 employees in 1933 to more than
6,500 today (1954). Through the years, more than 300 men
and a score of women, all ex-convicts, have gone to work
here at Brown & Bigelow upon their release from prison.
Many of them were paroled to me. A few of these men and
women have earned executive jobs with the company.
Others have remained loyal and hard-working factory
workers for as long as 20 years.

We haven't coddled them. Outside of giving them a
chance to hold a decent job, the only other extra benefit
they get is that we forget their past.

All kinds of criminals have come to us. Believing in
them, we help them to look forward, whatever they've
done. Thus, I have no worries about the murderer who
works on my farm, tending the garden where my three
children play. Everyone knows what he has done, but
everyone believes in what he is doing. Trust must be a
full-hearted thing, for you cannot help a man toward
whom you have reservations.

The help I've been able to give ex-convicts is no crusade.
But a crusade I do have is this: I'd like to see many more
employers realize it is not beneath their dignity to help those
who have transgressed. Rehabilitation of a man is accomplished on the outside, not on the inside of a prison wall.

Charles A. Ward

I'm requesting early parole so I can plug my new book.

Putting People First

Forrest King couldn't believe the scene. Dozens of Federal Express employees were cheering as he and his wife stepped out of the chartered Boeing 747 airplane. King had come to Memphis with other Flying Tiger employees, whose company had recently been bought by Federal Express, to see if he wanted to relocate. The welcome, complete with a red carpet and a welcoming committee that included the mayor of Memphis and FedEx's CEO, was King's introduction to this unusual company.

According to King: "It seems to me that when another company takes you over, they are not necessarily obligated to give you a job in the first place. But everyone— and it was communicated in a memo and later in video— was offered a job."

CEO Fred Smith's "people first" management style can be summed up by one of FedEx's slogans: "People, Service, Profit," or P-S-P. "Take care of our people; they, in turn, will deliver the impeccable service demanded by our customers, who will reward us with the profitability necessary to secure our future."

And FedEx does take care of its people. When the

company's Zapmail program was shut down in 1986, all 1,300 of the employees who had worked in that department had first priority in internal job posting applications. Those employees who could not find positions with equivalent salaries could take lower-level jobs and retain their previous salary for up to 15 months, or until they found another higher-salary job.

And when FedEx discontinued much of its service within Europe and reduced its European work force from 9,200 to 2,600, FedEx received praise from *The London Times,* among others, for the way in which it went about the layoffs. For example, FedEx put full-page ads in several newspapers urging other employers to hire former FedEx workers. In Belgium alone, 80 companies responded to the ad with a total of 600 job offers.

FedEx people stick together in hard times.

Robert Levering, Milton Moskowitz
and Michael Katz

True Stewardship

The true perfection of man lies not in what man has, but in what man is.

Oscar Wilde

I have always loved to work with machinery. The feel of a piece of steel, the magic of putting bolts and wire together fascinated me. Eventually I rigged myself up a little shop where I could tinker to my heart's content.

The automobile was invented, and I soon learned to take it apart and put it together, bolt by bolt. Except for the horn. Quite often I just couldn't make it work. I wanted to invent a horn that never failed to blow.

Then I got to thinking about my trombone, and the way the reeds in it were fitted together. This idea led to some experimentation, the result being a new horn called Gabriel's Horn, and a company to manufacture it. I started the Gabriel Company on $1,500 I had saved up.

Then the day came when I decided to sell my business. A big investment firm offered me $10 million. I was floored by this amount. True, the company was bringing in a large income, but it was all based on patents soon to expire. Therefore, I figured the business was not worth $10 million. If I sold at this price, many little stockholders in the purchasing firm might lose their money.

Over the years I have come to realize that nothing we earn, none of the things we accumulate, belongs to us. While on earth we are merely stewards or trustees for God's resources. Our job is to handle these resources as wisely as possible and to use what money we have for the good of the greatest number.

So I finally sold the company, but for $4 million instead of 10, which I thought was a fair price.

Then I had an idea to hold a party for my friends. Many of them had worked years to build up an orphanage, or raise money for a desperately needed new wing on a hospital, and other such causes. They wouldn't know about it in advance, but at the party I decided to give away to these wonderful people the $4 million God had entrusted to me.

Do you know, I actually felt a little selfish having as much fun as I did that night. It was the best party I ever had.

Claud H. Foster

"Thank You for Believing Me Well"

The real act of discovery is not in finding new lands, but in seeing with new eyes.

Marcel Proust

As a young social worker in a New York City psychiatric clinic, I was asked to see Roz, a 20-year-old woman who had been referred to us from another psychiatric facility. It was an unusual referral in that no information was received ahead of her first appointment. I was told to "play it by ear," and to figure out what her problems were and what she needed.

Without a diagnosis to go on, I saw Roz as an unhappy, misunderstood young woman who hadn't been listened to in her earlier therapy. Her family situation was unpleasant. I didn't see her as disturbed, but rather as lonely and misunderstood. She responded so positively to being heard. I worked with her to start a life worth living—to find a job, a satisfying place to live and new relationships. We hit it off well, and she started making important changes in her life right away.

The records from the previous psychiatric facility arrived a month after Roz and I began our successful work together. To my complete surprise, her records were several inches thick, describing a number of psychiatric hospitalizations. Her diagnosis was "paranoid schizophrenic," with a comment on her being "hopeless."

That had not been my experience with Roz at all. I decided to forget those pieces of paper. I never treated her as if she had that "hopeless" diagnosis. (It was a lesson for me in questioning the value and certainty of diagnoses.) I did find out about the horrors for Roz of those hospitalizations, of being drugged, isolated and abused. I also learned a lot from her about surviving such traumatic circumstances.

First Roz found a job, then a place to live away from her difficult family. After several months of working together, she introduced me to her husband-to-be, a successful businessman who adored her.

When we completed our therapy, Roz gave me the gift of a silver bookmark and a note that said, "Thank you for believing me well."

I have carried that note with me and I will for the rest of my life, to remind me of the stand I take for people, thanks to one brave woman's triumph over a "hopeless" diagnosis.

Judy Tatelbaum

An Act of Kindness

*Love cures people—both the ones who give it
and the ones who receive it.*

Dr. Karl Menninger

I was being interviewed by a senior manager for a
major insurance company. I told him honestly that the
principal reason that I was interviewing with them was
my need to keep my family in Boston. My wife of 26 years
had recently died of a heart attack. A job in Boston would
help me reduce some of the extreme trauma and pain of
the loss for my 16-year-old daughter. It was important to
me to keep her in her present high school.

I could still barely talk about the loss of my wife. Bruce,
the interviewer, was politely empathetic, but he didn't
probe any further. He acknowledged my loss and, with
great respect, moved on to another subject.

After the next round of interviews, Bruce took me to
lunch with another manager. Then he asked me to take a
walk with him. He told me that he, too, had lost his wife.
And, like me, he had also been married 20 years and had

three children. In his sharing, I realized that he had experienced the same pain as I had   a pain that was almost impossible to explain to someone who had not lost a loved one. He offered his business card and home phone number and suggested that, should I need help or just want someone to talk to, I should feel free to give him a call. Whether I got the job or not, he wanted me to know that he was there if I ever needed help.

From that one act of kindness, when he had no idea if we would ever see each other again, he helped our family deal with one of life's greatest losses. He turned the normally cold business interview process into an act of caring and support for another person in a time of extreme need.

Mike Teeley

The Power of Being Human

Life is an opportunity to contribute love in your own way.

Bernie Siegel, M.D.

With my graduate degree from Princeton and numerous public speaking honors packed in my bag, I arrived at a small-town church somewhere in Oklahoma and began giving them sermons as sparkling as my résumé.

The congregation's response was gracious and encouraging, but not all of them caught fire with the fervency I had in mind. Especially the deacons. Most of them were young, my age or slightly older. I decided they lacked the maturity to appreciate the seriousness of the eloquent challenge I laid before them.

There was one exception: Vilas Copple. Vilas was older— somewhere around 50, I'd guess. He looked like an oil field worker, which he was. I don't know exactly what Vilas did, but I suspect it was something that called for both the education that comes with experience and the endurance of hard physical labor. I do know that he cared about his church. He sang in the choir, attended Sunday school, and supported my efforts to light a fire under the deacons.

That was what Vilas and I discussed for almost an hour after the deacons' meeting one Monday evening. Then we parted to go home. As soon as I walked in the front door, the phone rang. It was Vilas. He'd arrived home and found his wife collapsed and dead on the kitchen floor. They'd eaten dinner together that evening, and she seemed to be in perfect health. But now this. Would I come over? Of course. It was my job.

I walked to Vilas's house, not only because it was relatively close, but also because I was in no hurry to get there. Every step of the way, frantic questions raced about in my head. What was I going to say? What could I do? How could I help? This wasn't like preparing a sermon. For the sermons, I had time and books to consult; other than my desire to be seen as a master of motivation, there was no desperate urgency attached to them. This was different. This was the real thing. A man's wife, his loved and loving companion, the mother of his children, was dead. This was as real as it gets. Although it was my job, I had nothing to say.

So that's what I did for most of the night. I said almost nothing. After the coroner had come and gone and the body was draped and taken away, Vilas and I sat there in his living room for hours, mostly in silence; both of us. There were a few barely audible prayers that were mostly whispered, fragmented sentences. He was not educated in the way of words, and I, confronted for the first time with a human being in critical need, had nothing to say.

Dawn was breaking when I returned home. One of the clearest memories of that entire night was looking at myself in the mirror as I brushed my teeth and saying, *What in the hell are you doing in this business?* I went to bed thinking about what other lines of work I could get into without going back for a lot more schooling. Nothing came to mind.

Some two years later I received a call to another church. I was excited to go, but it was also a time of sadness, parting with a congregation that had been so understanding and supportive of their young pastor. They had taught me a lot and graciously assured me I'd done the same for them. In looking back, I got the better deal.

Now it was the last Sunday, the last sermon. Even some of the choir, who usually went directly to the choir room to hang up their robes after the service, were in line to shake hands and share a hug with their departing pastor. I looked up and there was Vilas, big tears rolling down his rugged red face. Vilas took my hand in both of his, looked me straight in the eye, and said, "Bob, I could never have made it through that night without you."

There was no need to explain what he meant by "that night," but it was by no means immediately apparent why he couldn't have made it through that night without me. That was the night I'd felt totally unworthy and incapable of doing anything important or helpful, the night I was so painfully aware that I lacked the words and the power to function effectively in the midst of catastrophe, to penetrate the trauma with at least a glimmering of hope. But for Vilas, that was the night he couldn't have made it through without me. Why did we have such completely different memories?

The truth is that we simply are not always magnificently wise in the face of life's tragedies. There is only one thing wrong with that old saying, "I'm only human": It usually comes out sounding like an excuse, when it should be an affirmation, a glorious affirmation of our thanks and our worth.

Robert R. Ball

A Kind Word

We are here to help one another along life's journey.

William J. Bennett

In January of 1986 I was flipping through the channels on TV and saw the closing credits for a PBS broadcast called "Funny Business," a show about cartooning. I had always wanted to be a cartoonist but never knew how to go about it. I wrote to the host of the show, cartoonist Jack Cassady, and asked his advice on entering the profession.

A few weeks later, I got an encouraging handwritten letter from Jack, answering all of my specific questions about materials and process. He went on to warn me about the likelihood of being rejected at first, advising me not to get discouraged if that happened. He said the cartoon samples I had sent him were good and worthy of publication.

I got very excited, finally understanding how the whole process worked. I submitted my best cartoons to *Playboy* and *The New Yorker*. The magazines quickly rejected me with cold little photocopied form letters. Discouraged, I put my art supplies in the closet and decided to forget about cartooning.

In June of 1987—out of the blue—I got a second letter from Jack Cassady. This was surprising, since I hadn't even thanked him for the original advice. Here's what his letter said:

> *Dear Scott:*
>
> *I was reviewing my "Funny Business" mail file when I again ran across your letter and copies of your cartoons. I remember answering your letter.*
>
> *The reason I'm dropping you this note is to again encourage you to submit your ideas to various publications. I hope you have already done so and are on the road to making a few bucks and having some fun, too.*
>
> *Sometimes encouragement in the funny business of graphic humor is hard to come by. That's why I am encouraging you to hang in there and keep drawing.*
>
> *I wish you lots of luck, sales and good drawing.*
>
> *Sincerely,*
> *Jack*

I was profoundly touched by his letter, largely, I think, because Jack had nothing to gain—including my thanks, if history was any indication. I acted on his encouragement, dragged my art supplies out of storage and inked the sample strips that eventually became "Dilbert." Now, 700 newspapers and six books later, things are going pretty well in Dilbertville.

I feel certain that I wouldn't have tried cartooning again if Jack hadn't sent the second letter. With a kind word and a postage stamp, he started a chain of events that reaches all the way to you right now. As "Dilbert" became more successful, I came to appreciate the enormity of Jack's simple act of kindness. I did eventually thank him, but I could never shake the feeling that I had been given a gift that defied reciprocation. Somehow, thanks didn't seem to be enough.

Over time, I have come to understand that some gifts are meant to be passed on, not repaid. All of us know somebody who would benefit from a kind word. I'm encouraging you to act on it. For the biggest impact, do it in writing. And do it for somebody who knows you have nothing to gain.

It's important to give encouragement to family and friends, but their happiness and yours are inseparable. For the maximum velocity, I'm suggesting that you give your encouragement to someone who can't return the favor—it's a distinction that won't be lost on the recipient.

And remember, there's no such thing as a small act of kindness. Every act creates a ripple with no logical end.

Scott Adams (creator of "Dilbert")
Submitted by Andrew Shalit

DILBERT reprinted by permission from United Feature Syndicate, Inc.

The Youngest Cop
in Arizona

Compassion is the chief law of human existence.

Fyodor Dostoyevsky

Tommy Austin had a reputation. In his world, lies were routine. Everyone had an excuse and an angle. Tommy was a customs agent in Arizona. He had to be smart and tough—Tommy was both.

Chris was a scrawny seven-year-old, hospitalized for leukemia. He saw a simpler world. His heroes were Pancho and John. They were motorcycle cops who rode a television highway and made good things happen. Chris wanted to be one of them.

Chris's mom, Linda, was a single parent who had moved to Phoenix in the hope of a new and better life. The deck she played was new, but the hands got worse.

One evening Tommy was visiting a friend in the hospital where Chris was staying. Chris caught him off-guard with, "Stick-em-up. I'm a cop, and you're under arrest." As men do with kids, Tommy played along. As kids do with men, Chris returned imagination, innocence and trust. Tommy wanted to give a gift in return.

Tommy knew this scrawny kid could never be the cop of his dreams, but he dreamed of a way to make the kid a cop. He enlisted the help of a couple of highway patrolmen, Scott and Frank, a couple of women friends, his boss, and a commander in the Arizona Department of Public Safety.

On the first day, Chris rode in a real patrol car and turned on the siren. He flew in a police helicopter. He rode his miniature battery-powered police cycle and earned his "wings." He received a proclamation as "the first and only official seven-year-old policeman in Arizona." Two women stayed up all night to tailor a custom uniform. Chris lived his dream in three wondrously exciting days of glory and love.

On the fourth day, Chris asked his mom to bring his uniform to the hospital. Scott and Frank pinned on his motorcycle "wings," and that day, Chris died. There were those who thought that leukemia had tragically claimed another child victim—but it was a "cop" who died that day.

When Linda took him back east for burial, the body was accompanied by the Arizona Highway Patrol. "We bury our brothers," they said, and Chris had a policeman's funeral.

A quote from Lowell tells us, "It's not what we give but what we share." Tommy, patrolmen Scott and Frank, Chris's mom, Linda, and more than 11,000 volunteers in 82 chapters have shared in Chris's gift. The Make-A-Wish Foundation, formed in a grieving mother's kitchen, has granted more than 37,000 wishes for kids with life-threatening illness since 1980. Internationally, more than 3,000 other kids have experienced the legacy of "the first and only seven-year-old policeman in Arizona."

Michael Cody

3

THE POWER OF ACKNOWLEDGMENT

If the only prayer you say in your whole life is "thank you," that would suffice.

Meister Eckehart

Nonsense . . . after 25 years, you deserve it!

The Whale Story

Celebrate what you want to see more of.

Tom Peters

Have you ever wondered how the whale and porpoise trainers at Sea World get Shamu, the 19,000-pound whale, to jump 22 feet out of the water and perform tricks? They get that whale to go over a rope farther out of the water than most of us can imagine. This is a great challenge—as great as the ones you and I face as parents, coaches or managers.

Can you imagine the typical American managerial approach to this situation? The first thing we would do would be to get that rope right up there at 22 feet—no sense celebrating shortcomings. We call that goal-setting, or strategic planning. With the goal clearly defined, we now have to figure out a way to motivate the whale. So we take a bucket of fish and put it right above that 22-foot rope—don't pay the whale unless it performs. Then we have to give direction. We lean over from our nice high and dry perch and say, "Jump, whale!"

And the whale stays right where it is.

So how do the trainers at Sea World do it? Their number one priority is to reinforce the behavior that they want repeated—in this case, to get the whale or porpoise to go over the rope. They influence the environment every way they can so that it supports the principle of making sure that *the whale can't fail.* They start with the rope below the surface of the water, in a position where the whale can't help but do what's expected of it. Every time the whale goes over the rope, it gets positive reinforcement. It gets fed fish, patted, played with, and most important, it gets that reinforcement.

But what happens when the whale goes *under* the rope? Nothing—no electric shock, no constructive criticism, no developmental feedback and no warnings in the personnel file. Whales are taught that their negative behavior will not be acknowledged.

Positive reinforcement is the cornerstone of that simple principle that produces such spectacular results. And as the whale begins to go over the rope more often than under, the trainers begin to raise the rope. It must be raised slowly enough so that the whale doesn't starve, either physically or emotionally.

The simple lesson to be learned from the whale trainers is to *over-celebrate.* Make a big deal out of the good and little stuff that we want consistently. Secondly, *under-criticize.* People know when they screw up. What they need is help. If we under-criticize, punish and discipline less than is expected, people will not forget the event and usually will not repeat it.

In my opinion, most successful businesses today are doing things right more than 95 percent of the time. Yet what do we spend the majority of our time giving feedback on? That's right—the 2, 3, 4, maybe even the 5 percent of things that we don't want repeated and didn't want to happen in the first place.

We need to set up the circumstances so that people can't fail. Over-celebrate, under-criticize . . . and know how far to raise the rope.

Charles A. Coonradt

Rich Beyond Measure

The greatest good you can do for another is not just to share your riches, but to reveal to him his own.

Benjamin Disraeli

Today I feel rich beyond measure. What began as a new idea for my department's celebration of the holiday season has become a very moving and enriching experience.

I was tired of the usual "draw names and buy a joke gift for under $15" way of holiday celebration, so I proposed that we try something different. "How about giving each other the gift of acknowledgment?" I asked. Everyone agreed; they were even enthusiastic. A few days before Christmas, six of us gathered in my office. To start, I asked that we all observe a few ground rules. The person whose turn it was to be acknowledged could only say "thank you." I also pointed out that it might be natural to feel uncomfortable giving and receiving acknowledgment, but if some people were truly uncomfortable, they could ask for their acknowledgment in private. Silence and pauses were deemed to be all right. They were probably just opportunities to let the good stuff sink in.

As we began our process, it struck me that the tribes and communities that pass their cultures along through storytelling are very wise people. Invariably, whoever was speaking would tell a story that illustrated the acknowledgment he or she wanted to make.

Each of us started our communication by saying to our colleague, "(Name), the gift you give to me is . . ." As each group member spoke to the person being acknowledged, I began to see sides of my colleagues of which I wasn't aware. One male staffer acknowledged another male for his state of grace that shone through. Another said, "I rest easy knowing you are the one in your position." Other comments included: "You give me the gift of your patience," "You listen to me," "I knew the moment I met you that I belonged here," and so on. It was a privilege to be there.

The spirit and connectedness we shared for those 60 minutes became bigger than we were. When we finished, no one wanted to speak; we didn't want to break the spell. It had been woven with heartfelt, authentic, simple truths that we had shared with each other. We were all humbled and enriched by it.

I believe we will always treasure the gifts we gave each other that day. I know how priceless my own acknowledgments were for me. It cost each of us nothing but our willingness to see the gifts in others and to speak it out loud.

Christine Barnes

Managing from the Heart

Hear and understand me.
Even if you disagree, please don't make me wrong.
Acknowledge the greatness within me.
Remember to look for my loving intentions.
Tell me the truth with compassion.

Hyler Bracey, Jack Rosenblum,
Aubrey Sanford and Roy Trueblood

Trucks and Trust

Trust men and they will be true to you; treat them greatly and they will show themselves great.

Ralph Waldo Emerson

"Preston was just like all the other trucking companies," Sales Vice-President Paul Sims told us. "Management knew all the answers. If there was a question, management would make the judgment. No matter that the manager had seven years' experience, and the driver had 20. The feeling was, 'I am the manager. I have the title.' When a guy didn't have the right attitude, I would give him workloads to straighten him out."

Then in 1978, Will Potter arrived as CEO of Preston, the Maryland-based company. Potter announced to management—and the drivers—that *management* was the problem. Paul Sims was then an assistant manager in the Canton, Ohio, terminal. He admits he thought Potter "was nuts," but he decided to hang around and give the new approach a try. (A lot of other managers bailed out.)

After a seminar on "performance management," for example, Sims bought an easel and started posting how productive we were—posting revenues and load averages. He was taken aback when drivers immediately started asking questions. "I'd show them their productivity for the day, and I'd draw a star or use a sticker when they did a good job," he recalls. "I saw these grown guys getting excited about this. If I got real busy in the morning and didn't put the figures up, the guys would come over to me and say, 'Sims! Put those figures up!'" All the involvement nearly wore Sims out. It got to the point where he was coming in at four in the morning and leaving at six at night, exhausted.

"So one day, I had three keys made to the terminal," he continued. "The morning shift came in, and I put the keys down on the table. 'What's that for?' they asked.

"'So that you can unlock the door in the morning,' I said.

"'What? You aren't going to be here?'

"I said, 'No, I can't keep coming in at 4:00 A.M. You guys work 4:30 A.M. to 1:00 P.M., but I have to stay until six—and it's killing me.' And they asked, 'What if we have a problem?'

"'Solve it,' I said.

"'What if we can't?'

"I said, 'Here's my number at home; call and wake me up.'

"'You trust us?'

"'I wouldn't have made these keys if I didn't,' I said. "They couldn't believe it."

Tom Peters

What makes you think I don't trust you, Phillips?

Reprinted with permission from Harley Schwadron.

A Lady Named Lill

Kind words can be short and easy to speak, but their echoes are truly endless.

Mother Teresa

Lillian was a young French Canadian girl who grew up in the farming community of River Canard, Ontario. At the age of 16, her father thought "Lill" had had enough schooling, and she was forced to drop out of school to contribute to the family income. In 1922, with English as her second language and limited education and skills, the future didn't look bright for Lill.

Her father, Eugene Bezaire, was a stern man who rarely took no for an answer and never accepted excuses. He demanded that Lill find a job. But her limitations left her with little confidence and low self-esteem, and she didn't know what work she could do.

With small hope of gaining employment, she would still ride the bus daily into the "big cities" of Windsor or Detroit. But she couldn't muster the courage to respond to a Help Wanted ad; she couldn't even bring herself to knock on a door. Each day she would just ride to the city, walk aimlessly about and at dusk return home. Her father would ask, "Any luck today, Lill?"

"No . . . no luck today, Dad," she would respond meekly.

As the days passed, Lill continued to ride and her father continued to ask about her job-hunting. The questions became more demanding, and Lill knew she would soon have to knock on a door.

On one of her trips, Lill saw a sign at the Carhartt Overall Company in downtown Detroit. "HELP WANTED," the sign said, "SECRETARIAL. APPLY WITHIN."

She walked up the long flight of stairs to the Carhartt Company offices. Cautiously, Lill knocked on her very first door. She was met by the office manager, Margaret Costello. In her broken English, Lill told her she was interested in the secretarial position, falsely stating that she was 19. Margaret knew something wasn't right, but decided to give the girl a chance.

She guided Lill through the old business office of the Carhartt Company. With rows and rows of people seated at rows and rows of typewriters and adding machines, Lill felt as if a hundred pairs of eyes were staring at her. With her chin on her chest and her eyes staring down, the reluctant farm girl followed Margaret to the back of the somber room. Margaret sat her down at a typewriter and said, "Lill, let's see how good you really are."

She directed Lill to type a single letter, and then left. Lill looked at the clock and saw that it was 11:40 A.M. Everyone would be leaving for lunch at noon. She figured that she could slip away in the crowd then. But she knew she should at least attempt the letter.

On her first try, she got through one line. It had five words, and she made four mistakes. She pulled the paper out and threw it away. The clock now read 11:45. "At noon," she said to herself, "I'll move out with the crowd, and they will never see me again."

On her second attempt, Lill got through a full paragraph, but still made many mistakes. Again she pulled out the paper, threw it out and started over. This time she completed the letter, but her work was still strewn with errors. She looked at the clock: 11:55—five minutes to freedom.

Just then, the door at one end of the office opened and Margaret walked in. She came directly over to Lill, putting one hand on the desk and the other on the girl's shoulder. She read the letter and paused. Then she said, "Lill, you're doing good work!"

Lill was stunned. She looked at the letter, then up at Margaret. With those simple words of encouragement, her desire to escape vanished and her confidence began to grow. She thought, "Well, if she thinks it's good, then it must be good. I think I'll stay!"

Lill did stay at Carhartt Overall Company . . . for 51 years, through two world wars and a Depression, through 11 presidents and six prime ministers—all because someone had the insight to give a shy and uncertain young girl the gift of self-esteem when she knocked on the door.

Dedicated to Lillian Kennedy by James M. Kennedy (son)
and James C. Kennedy (grandson)

"Your Work Is Recognized!"

*There'll be pennies from heaven for you and
me.*

John Burke

It all began in Everett, Washington, where my project
team was in the process of implementing one of our business systems. One morning, as I walked through the
parking lot with one of my employees, I found a penny
and picked it up. Playfully, I presented the penny to the
employee and said, "This is a discretionary award for
your efforts." He put the penny in his pocket. "Thank
you," he said.

About six months later, I was walking with the same
employee, this time in Los Alamitos, California, when I
again found a penny and gave it to him.

Later, I had an occasion to go into his office and there,
taped on a piece of paper, were the two pennies. He said he
was displaying them as his recognition for a job well done.

Other employees noticed the pennies proudly displayed and began asking why they hadn't received any.

So I started handing out pennies, explaining that they were for recognition, not for reward. Soon, so many people wanted them that I designed a penny holder. The front features a place for a penny and beside it the phrase, "Your work is recognized!" The back has slots for 30 more pennies and the phrase, "Your achievements count!"

One time, I spotted an employee doing something right and wanted to recognize her, but I didn't have a penny, so I gave her a quarter. Later that same day she stopped by and returned 24 cents.

That's how the "Prestigious Penny Award" was born. It's become a significant source of recognition in our organization.

Gary Hruska

"It's our new employee recognition award."

Two Ripe Bananas

Take time to marvel at the wonders of life.

Gary W. Fenchuk

Pat Beck is an artist whose medium is mud. More precisely, adobe—a mixture of mud and straw, from which she sculpts enchanting figures of primordial elegance. Like many artists, she lives between a rock and a hard place, or in her case, mud and a mud-hole, occasionally supplementing her income with other work.

In 1994, she and a friend, Holly, were hired to assist in a community art project in the small town of Magdalena, New Mexico. Magdalena is a community in the Gallinas Mountains on the edge of the great plain of St. Augustine. Once a mining and railroad center, Magdalena's population has now dwindled to about 1,000.

Pat and Holly were given a plot of land near the remnants of the cattle pens, a vestige of Magdalena's heyday as a cattle center, to begin their project. With the help of the community, Holly created two large cows and a cowboy. They were made entirely of found objects like old wagon parts, used baling wire donated by the nearby ranchers, and even a rusted shotgun barrel dug up in someone's yard. Pat taught the high school students how to make adobe bricks, and from these, Pat and the community created an adobe wall. The elementary-school children were invited to make a personal shape out of mud, and these were used as decorative relief.

As the wall began to take shape, many of the adults and children stopped by to check on its progress, and they were invited to put their handprints, brands and initials on the wall. As a final touch, earth colors were gathered from the Navajo reservation, a big part of the history of the area, and added to the wall. All in all, over 300 people contributed to the project.

One of Pat's daily visitors was a retired miner, Gene. Almost every day he would bring something to help her understand the glory days of mining—a picture, samples of ore from the mine, an old newspaper article.

One day when the wall was almost finished, Gene arrived for his usual visit. In a moment of inspiration, Pat sculpted the face of a miner into the wall. Gene had given her a piece of shiny ore, and Pat made this the light in the miner's helmet. When she was finished, she wrote Gene's name under the head of the miner. They both stood back and admired her creation. Then without a word, Gene turned and left. Pat wasn't sure if he had been offended in some way, but 10 minutes later he came back with two ripe bananas. Again without a word, he put them on the wall where she was working and left.

Pat has received and will continue to receive many tributes to her work. But I doubt there will ever be one as meaningful as those two ripe bananas.

Maida Rogerson

The Scrapbook

Life is to be fortified by many friendships. To love and to be loved is the greatest happiness.

Sydney Smith

Teaching English in Japan has been incredibly rewarding. I came here out of a longing for adventure and travel, and for a little relaxation. Miraculously, I've achieved all that and more. I've traveled all over the main island of Honshu, filled the pages of five journals, read over 60 books, written four short stories, and made friends with teachers and scholars from all over the world. I've been able to receive and had the chance to give back.

But my heart lies with my students—the businessmen who are being transferred to America, the housewives who want to expand their horizons, the high school students whose fondest wish is to attend a university in the States.

Over the course of the year that I have taught, I've often wondered who was the student and who was the teacher. The pupils nurtured and comforted me, helping me to better understand the Japanese culture. They applauded when I struggled with my first *hiragana* letters. They accompanied me to grocery store after grocery store, where I searched for three months to find peanut butter. They showed me how to fold paper into an *origami* swan and took me on riverboat rides. They invited me to traditional tea ceremonies, and over *omisoka,* the Japanese New Year, they took me into their homes, where they prepared meals in my honor. They also took me to the temple and taught me how to select a fortune; then they quickly gathered around, crying, "You have much good fortune! You big lucky!"

The last few weeks, as I've made preparations to return home, have been jam-packed with *sayonara* parties and gifts. So many students have showered me with presents: purses of handwoven silk, jewelry boxes, designer handkerchiefs, jade earrings and gold-trimmed china plates. We've sung ourselves hoarse at *karaoke,* hugged, held hands and exchanged countless good-byes. And through it all, I've managed to keep my emotions in check. Instead, I've let *them* shed the tears while I comforted them with promises to write.

Tonight is my last night to teach, and I'm ending it on an exceptionally high note with my favorite class. They're the advanced students, and over the year, we've engaged in political discussions, learned slang, role-played and done something rare among different cultures—we've laughed at one another's jokes.

While I'm preparing for this last class, Mika, the school manager, calls me to the front lobby. I enter the room and see the staff and several students standing around, hands clasped in eager anticipation. All eyes are turned in my direction. Mika has one last gift for me.

I carefully unwrap the paper, as the presentation of the gift is as important as the gift itself. The wrapper slowly slides off, and I see that she has given me a scrapbook. She tells me she prepared it just last night after weeks of collaborating with the students. I see the redness in her eyes. I open the cover.

Filling the pages are recent snapshots of all my students. Beside the pictures are personal notes written by them on small, colorful squares of paper. They've decorated the papers with hearts, smiles, little cat faces and neon-colored lines, stars, dots and triangles.

I know the challenge my students face in stringing together even simple phrases, and as I read, the dam of emotions I've been holding back begins to crack.

> *Thank you for your kindley teach.*
> *I had interesting class. Now maybe someday I go to America.*
> *I am forget to you.*
> *I've been enjoying to study English.*
> *Thank you for everything you did me. I very sad you go to America.*
> *Please don't forget memories in Japan.*

My tears begin to fall. I grope for words that have flowed so easily over the last year. My hands lightly touch the pages, and I outline their faces with my fingertips. I close the cover and wrap the book in my arms, holding it tightly to my heart.

The scrapbook has captured them forever. I may be leaving, but I'm taking each one of them back with me to America.

Gina Maria Jerome

A Coach with Soul

The size of your body is of little account; the size of your brain is of much account; the size of your heart is of the most account of all.

B.C. Forbes

In the late 1940s, in Cincinnati, Ohio, there was a little boy who wanted to be on the "pee wee" football team at his parochial elementary school. The minimum weight requirement was 70 pounds. The little boy struggled to put on the necessary pounds. The coach knew how much the little boy wanted to make the team, so he encouraged him to "bulk up" on weigh-in day by eating lots of bananas and drinking lots of malts. The boy soon tipped the scales at $69^1/2$ pounds, was given the benefit of the doubt, and put on the team roster.

Throughout the season, the coach benched the little guy for his own sake. The upper weight limit for the league was 120 pounds and he didn't want him to get injured. However, in the final game of the season, the team was short a few players and the coach had to play the little boy in order to avoid a forfeit. The coach played him at safety on defense, figuring the little boy would be out of most of the heavy hitting plays. Wouldn't you know it, on the last play of the game, the fullback from the other team broke through the line, eluded the secondary, and was bearing down on the little boy.

As the little boy peered through his helmet, which was too large and kept falling down in front of his eyes, he saw the approaching runner. He crouched down to try to get ready to tackle the big 120-pound bruiser. As the runner got closer, all the little boy could say to himself was, *this guy's got hair on his legs!* Here he was, barely 70 pounds, trying to tackle this big hairy guy. At the moment of truth, he reached out for the fullback's legs, grabbed onto one of them, and held on for dear life as the big bruiser dragged the little tot with him down the field. All the little boy could see was the infield dirt as his helmet banged on the ground all the way into the end zone.

Completely mortified by the experience, the boy fought back tears and the feeling he had let the team down. To his dismay, the coach and the whole team ran onto the field to congratulate him! The coach praised him for never giving up and for not letting the big guy scare him away from making the tackle. His teammates carried him off on their shoulders and then voted him the "gutsiest player of the game."

The coach's name is Dan Finley and the little boy was me.

In his youth, Dan, now in his 40s, had been a superb athlete with major league baseball potential. But Dan was stricken with polio, and was only able to walk with leg braces and a cane. He decided to turn his energy to coaching kids. The joy of playing had been taken from him prematurely, and he wanted to help kids make the most of their days on the playing field. He is still doing it.

Darrell J. Burnett, Ph.D.

4

SERVICE: SETTING NEW STANDARDS

*Work done in the true spirit of service . . .
is considered as worship.*

*Baha Allah
founder of the Baha'i faith*

Banking at Its Best

Great opportunities to help others seldom come, but small ones surround us daily.

Sally Koch

When my son was a young teenager, he and his friend set out on a bus across town to purchase skateboard axles. They each had $20. When they arrived downtown, they discovered they needed more money to cover bus fare and sales tax. They were short $3.75.

A branch of our bank was nearby, so they decided to go in and take out a loan. The teller told them that was not possible, but that they could get a cash advance on their parents' credit card. So they called home, but got no answer. They tried the teller again to see if anything more could be done. She referred them to the desk of the vice president. When he asked why the bank should give them a loan, they answered, "Because we're Boy Scouts and good students, and very trustworthy." He said that since they had no collateral, they would have to write out and sign an IOU. They did, and he in turn gave them the money they needed to complete their mission.

We found out later that this wonderful man lent the boys his own money. (My husband called him the next day asking for the same terms on a home loan!) In talking with the man, we learned that he had made many such loans, including a large one to a Navy wife whose allotment was delayed. He said he's been repaid almost 100 percent of the time, and that the opportunity to help others in this way was one of the most rewarding parts of his job.

My son and his friend hopped on the bus the very next morning. They paid off their loan and received their IOU signed by the vice president. It was banking at its best.

Sharon Borjesson

A Passionate Flight Attendant

Do what you love and love what you're doing,
and you'll never work another day in your life.
                                                Source Unknown

"Good morning, ladies and gentlemen. Welcome aboard United Airlines flight number 548, direct from Palm Springs to Chicago."

Wait a minute! My mind starts racing. I know it's early in the morning, 6:50 A.M. to be exact, but I was sure this flight went to Denver.

"Now that I got your attention," the voice continues, "my name is Annamarie and I'll be your first flight attendant today. Actually, we will be en route to Denver, so if you were not planning to go there, now would be a good time to get off the plane."

I breathe a sigh of relief as Annamarie continues: "Safety is important to us, so please take out the safety card in front of you and acquaint yourself with it. Come on, everybody, take out those brochures and wave them in the air!"

Seventy percent of the passengers chuckle and do as they are told, 20 percent aren't awake yet, and the other 10 percent are sourpusses.

"In the event that we mistakenly land in a body of water, a decision must be made. You can either pray and swim like crazy, or use your seat as a flotation device."

About half of the 20 percent start to emerge from their stupor. "We will be serving breakfast in flight this morning. On the menu I have eggs Benedict and fruit crêpes— not really, but they sound good to me. However, the flight attendants will be offering you a choice of an omelet or cold cereal."

By now, even a few of the sourpusses are venturing a smile. Thanks for an enjoyable flight, Annamarie. And thank God for flight attendants who are passionate about their jobs!

Glenn Van Ekeren

The "Bizarro" cartoon by Dan Piraro is reprinted courtesy Chronicle Features, San Francisco, California.

The Massage Is the Message

The only real way to differentiate yourself from the competition is through service.

Jonathan Tisch

I like to cook. I especially like to cook when there's nothing at stake: no guests to entertain, no relatives coming to dinner. Then I throw a little of this and a little of that into a pot, and if it doesn't turn out, it's just Pepto-Bismol for two and a couple of poached eggs on toast.

But this was Thanksgiving—Thanksgiving in a new country, a new city and with new friends. This was important—so important that I had even prepared much of the dinner ahead of time. By Thanksgiving day I was feeling a little smug. Pies were made, the turkey stuffed, sweet potatoes casseroled, and the house in that once-a-year state of cleanliness. Then in the early afternoon, I received a call reminding me that two of my guests were vegetarian. I'm sure they could have survived on the vegetables and salads I had prepared, but I was feeling so ahead of the game that I decided that while my turkey was roasting, I'd make a quick trip to Alfalfa's, one of our local vegetarian markets, to pick up a vegetarian entrée.

We live in the country. On a busy day, a car goes by our house once every hour, so I was ill-prepared for the number of people in town who also had last-minute shopping to do. Traffic was snarled and drivers snarling. I was starting to run late, and I hadn't even been able to get into the store's parking lot! But the minute I did, everything changed.

The manager of the store was in the lot, directing traffic and showing people where there were empty spaces. I parked and rushed into the store. Inside, store personnel were everywhere, handing out tidbits of food, offering suggestions, and helping people find what they were looking for. I quickly got what I needed; but even though all the cash registers were open, the lines were very long. I could feel my teeth clench at the thought of my guests arriving to a burnt turkey and no hostess.

The gentleman in front of me was also experiencing some panic, or so I thought, because an attractive woman was massaging his neck and shoulders. "What a lucky guy," I thought. Just then, the woman turned and said, "Would you like a neck and shoulder massage while you're waiting in line?" Would I! As she worked on me and I began to breathe again, I thought, "Isn't this great? An enterprising massage therapist plying her trade where she is most needed." When she finished, I asked her how much I owed her. "No, no," she said, "the massages are courtesy of the store."

Now I ask you, was that inspired service or what? The rest of the day was a piece of cake, or pumpkin pie if you will. And the dinner, on a scale of 1 to 10? About a 14.

Maida Rogerson

Not on the Menu

What do we live for if not to make the world less difficult for each other.

George Eliot

I travel a lot in my work, and one of the things I dislike about this part of my job is eating alone. It always makes me feel lonely to see others laughing and talking, and sometimes I have the uncomfortable feeling that I look like I am waiting to be "picked up" by someone. So, I usually order room service for several nights to avoid that discomfort. However, sooner or later, I feel a need to get out of my room. My strategy is to go down to the hotel restaurant the moment it opens, as it is not very crowded then and I don't feel as uncomfortable.

After having room service three nights in a row at a Wyndham Hotel in Houston, I needed to get out. Although the restaurant opened at 6:30, I arrived at 6:25. The maître d' met me at the front and made a comment

Excerpted from her book, *Care Packages for the Workplace: Dozens of Little Things You Can Do to Regenerate Spirit at Work.* McGraw Hill, ©1996.

about my "really being there early." I explained my dislike of eating alone in restaurants. He then took me back and seated me at a lovely table. "You know," he said, "I am all caught up with my work, and people don't usually start coming to our restaurant until after seven o'clock. I wondered if you'd mind if I sat down with you for a while."

I was delighted! He sat and talked with me about his career goals, his hobbies, the challenges of balancing a restaurant career with a family, and the difficulty of being at work on nights, weekends and holidays. He showed me pictures of his children and his wife—even his dog! After about 15 minutes, he spotted some customers at the front desk and excused himself. I noticed out of the corner of my eye that before he went to the front, he stopped in the kitchen for a moment.

As my new friend proceeded to seat the arriving party, one of the waiters came out of the kitchen and over to my table. "My station is way in the back tonight, and I'm sure no one will be seated there for a while," he said. "I'm not really busy. Do you mind if I sit down with you for a while?" We had a wonderful chat, until someone was seated in his station and he needed to excuse himself.

Soon after, out came one of the young busboys. He, too, asked if he could sit down with me for a few minutes. He hardly spoke any English, but I had taught English as a second language, so we had great fun talking about his experiences in coming to America. He shared with me all the expressions they had taught him in the kitchen when he first arrived in this country (you can imagine!). As the restaurant got busier, he finally excused himself to attend to his work. But before I left that night, even the chef had come out of the kitchen and sat with me!

When I asked for my check (about one and a half hours later), there was an almost audible pause in the restaurant. All the people who had sat down with me came over in a big group to my table. They presented me with a long-stemmed red rose and said, "This was the nicest night we've ever had in our restaurant." And I cried! What had begun as a lonely night ended as a beautiful experience—for both employees *and* customer.

Barbara Glanz

"Let's Start Over"

Do it big, do it right and do it with style.

Fred Astaire

Some time ago, I had a direct experience of what I describe as "High Performance Customer Service." It occurred on a Saturday, on a cold winter's day in Toronto.

The weekend began, as with many other second-family situations, with my children visiting their mother. My wife, Kate, and I had a weekend alone. Saturday was an exercise in leisure and tranquillity. We got up late, and everything in the day was a pleasurable three or four hours late.

After browsing shops and galleries, we arrived at a prominent four-star hotel at around four o'clock in the afternoon, ready for a late lunch. The restaurant staff was most accommodating. Kate ordered a stir-fry of some sort, and when it arrived, the real adventure began.

Nestled neatly in Kate's stir-fry was the tip of a finger from a latex glove. I called the waitress. "What is this?" Kate inquired with an appropriate level of indignation.

"I'm not sure," replied the waitress as she whisked the plate away to the kitchen.

In less than a minute the waitress returned with the maître d'. "Madame, we have made a dreadful mistake and apologize sincerely." So far so good. "Let us start over," the maître d' continued. "Remove everything from the table," he instructed the waitress. The waitress proceeded to remove everything—the wine, the cutlery, my food, the tablecloth—everything! "Let us erase the memory," said the maître d'.

The table was reset, menus presented, and new wine and food ordered. We were on our way once again to a fantastic lunch.

The maître d' took a bad service impression and replaced it with an outstanding one. He did not deny the experience, but substituted a higher, richer one in its place. The food was good, the service superlative. This was theater.

And the meal was complimentary.

Richard Porter

"Ah, Bambini!"

Kindness is the insignia of a loving heart.

Anonymous

My husband and I were traveling in Italy with two small babies and an au pair. We would trade sightseeing time with the au pair so we could all visit the requisite churches and museums. But on this day we took the babies along, since we had only one day to go to Assisi, and all of us urgently wanted to see it. The morning was wonderful—feeling like happy pilgrims, we read each other stories of St. Francis while the babies cooed and gurgled as we drove up the winding streets.

But by the end of a very hot day, traipsing uphill and downhill in the 90-degree Italian sun, the two kids were crying nonstop. One was throwing up; the other had diarrhea. We were all irritable and exhausted, and we had a three-hour trip ahead of us to get back to Florence, where we were staying. Somewhere on the plains of Perugia we stopped at a little trattoria to have dinner.

Embarrassed at our bedraggled state and our smelly,

noisy children, we sheepishly tried to sneak into the dining room, hoping we could silence the children long enough to order before they threw us out. The proprietor took one look at us, muttered, "You wait-a-here," and went back to the kitchen. We thought perhaps we should leave right then, but before we could decide what to do, he reappeared with his wife and teenage daughter. Beaming as they crossed the dining room, the two women threw out their arms, cried, "Ah, bambini!" and took the children from our arms, motioning us to sit at a quiet corner table.

For the duration of a long and hospitable dinner, they walked the babies back and forth in the back of the dining room, cooing, laughing and singing them to sleep in gentle, musical Italian. The proprietor even insisted we stay and have an extra glass of wine after the babies were asleep!

Any parent who has reached the end of his or her rope with an infant will appreciate that God had indeed sent us angels that day.

Editors of Conari Press

Beyond Order-Taking

*Hold yourself responsible for a higher standard
than anybody else expects of you.*

Henry Ward Beecher

Back in 1987, I was preparing to give a speech to a conference for seafood department managers of supermarkets. Lacking any good stories about the seafood business, I decided to go as a "mystery shopper" to my local grocery store and see if I could "create" a situation that might result in a colorful story.

As I neared the glass casing of the seafood department, a voice called out, "How can I help you?"

I'm thinking, *He doesn't realize, it's time for a pop quiz.* So I say, "You know, I'm very health-conscious. I realize that certain species of seafood are high in cholesterol and others are low in cholesterol. Could you tell me which ones?"

The seafood specialist said, "Sir, do you realize there are two kinds of cholesterol?" He proceeded to launch into a clear and helpful medical explanation of the differences between high-density lipoproteins and low-density lipoproteins. I was certain I was witnessing the second coming of Marcus Welby, M.D.

Although startled by his response, I persisted in administering my test of product knowledge. "I need more variety in my seafood preparation. Here I am living in Seattle, where we have such great seafood, but I don't know many recipes. Please understand, I'm busy, so help me find something easy to put together."

The seafood specialist walked briskly out from behind the counter and gestured with his hand in a way that said, "Follow me." We headed into the grocery aisles to the spice section. He reached up to the top shelf, pulled off a box and held it up, saying, "This spice from Japan is excellent. Very versatile. Goes well with any seafood. This is a good place to start."

As we walked back to the seafood department, he stopped just before the glass casing, looked me square in the eyes and said, "Sir, let me be sure I understand your needs. You're saying you want healthy seafood and a variety of recipes that don't take much time to prepare?"

I said, "Yes, precisely."

"Have I got a book for you." He pulled down a book and put the front cover about 10 inches from my eyes. The title read, *Healthy, Easy-to-Prepare Seafood Recipes for the Pacific Northwest.*

As I thumbed through the pages, the recipe titles sounded delicious. Forgetting my purpose for this mystery shopping trip, I couldn't resist placing orders. Salmon . . . halibut . . . tuna . . . scallops! I was on a roll.

As I pushed my shopping cart toward the checkout stand, the irony of the situation dawned on me. I had come to the seafood department to test this guy's product knowledge, to get a good story for a speech. I was leaving with what was, for me, an all-time record for seafood purchases in a single shopping trip.

The seafood specialist was far more than an order-taker. He was an extraordinary problem-solver who made a difference in the quality of my seafood dinners, and who made me feel like the most important shopper in the store that day. If there were a Supermarket Hall of Fame, my seafood-filled shopping cart would have been a resounding vote of confidence for this dedicated worker.

Art Turock

"Welcome to Venetia"

Caring is a powerful business advantage.

Scott Johnson

I'd been driving for seven hours, was tired of the road, and decided to stop for the night before going on to San Francisco. The hotel was located in a redwood grove overlooking the Pacific. The minute I walked into the lobby, something told me that I was in a special place.

The lobby was warmly lighted. A long, dark wood table faced the front door. On it rested a huge woven Indian basket overflowing with fresh fruit. Against the far wall, in a massive fieldstone fireplace, a roaring fire filled the room with its cheerful crackling.

"Welcome to Venetia," the receptionist said from behind the reception desk. It took no more than three minutes from the moment she spoke that greeting to the time the bellboy ushered me into my room, despite the fact that I had no reservation.

And the room! Thick, muted pastel, wall-to-wall carpeting; a four-poster, king-size, white pine bed covered with a magnificent, white-on-white quilt; original graphics depicting scenes and birds of the Pacific Northwest; a stone fireplace with oak logs already prepared and waiting on the grate—all created an atmosphere of understated elegance.

When I returned from dinner, I looked forward to a fire and possibly a brandy before going to bed.

Someone had beaten me to it.

A brisk fire was burning in the fireplace. The quilt was turned down on the bed. The pillows were plumped up, a mint resting on each one. On one of the night tables beside the bed stood a glass of brandy and a card that read:

> *Welcome to your first stay at Venetia. I hope it has been enjoyable. If there is anything I can do for you, day or night, please don't hesitate to call.*
>
> *Kathi*

As I drifted to sleep that evening, I felt very well taken care of.

The following morning I awoke to a strange bubbling sound in the bathroom. A pot of coffee, turned on by an automatic timer, was perking away on the sink counter. And it was my brand of coffee! How in the world could they have known that? And then I remembered that in the hotel restaurant the night before, they had asked me which brand of coffee I preferred.

There was a polite knock on the door. I opened the door and on the mat was a newspaper. *My newspaper.* I remembered when I had checked in the night before, the receptionist had asked me which newspaper I preferred; I hadn't given it another thought.

This exact same scenario has occurred each and every time I've returned to the Venetia, with one exception.

After the first time, I was never asked my preferences again. I had become a part of the hotel's management system. And never once has it let me down.

Michael E. Gerber

The "Bizarro" cartoon by Dan Piraro is reprinted courtesy Chronicle Features, San Francisco, California.

Customer Service Is Not a Mickey Mouse Affair

Not too long ago, a guest checking out of our Polynesian Village resort at Walt Disney World was asked how she enjoyed her visit. She told the front-desk clerk she had had a wonderful vacation, but was heartbroken about losing several rolls of Kodacolor film she had not yet developed. She was particularly upset over the loss of the pictures she had shot at our Polynesian Luau, as this was a memory she especially treasured.

Now, please understand that we have no written service standards covering lost luau snapshots. Fortunately, the hostess at the front desk understood Disney's philosophy of caring for our guests. She asked the woman to leave her a couple of rolls of fresh film, promising she would take care of the rest.

Two weeks later, this guest received a package at her home. In it were photos of the entire cast of our luau show, personally autographed by each performer. There were also photos of the parade and fireworks in the theme park, taken by the front-desk hostess on her own time, after work. I happen to know this story because this guest wrote us a letter. She said that never in her life had she received such compassionate service from any business establishment.

Heroic service does not come from policy manuals. It comes from people who care—and from a culture that encourages and models that attitude.

Valerie Oberle
vice president
Disney University Guest Programs

Pass It On

*We are prone to judge success by the index of
our salaries or the size of our automobiles rather
than by the quality of our service and relationship to mankind.*

Martin Luther King Jr.

There I was with my wife and our two-year-old daughter, in an isolated, snow-packed campground in Oregon's
Rogue River Valley, with a comatose vehicle. We were on
a journey to celebrate the completion of my second year
of residency training, but my recently acquired medical
savvy was of no use to the recreational vehicle we had
rented for the trip.

This happened 20 years ago, but I remember it as
clearly as I do the cloudless Oregon sky. I had just awakened, fumbled around with the light switch, and been
greeted with darkness. I tried the ignition. No response.
As I climbed out of the camper, fortunately my profanities
were drowned out in the roar of the white-water rapids.

My wife and I concluded that we were victims of a

dead battery and that my legs were of more value than my automotive knowledge. I decided to hike back to the main highway, several miles away, while she stayed with our daughter.

Two hours and a twisted ankle later, I arrived at the highway and flagged down a logging truck, which let me off at the first gas station we came to and drove off. As I approached the station, I had the sinking realization that it was Sunday morning. The place was closed. But there was a pay phone and a tattered phone book. I called the only automotive service company located in the next town, some 20 miles away.

Bob answered and listened as I explained my predicament. "No problem," he said as I gave my location. "I'm usually closed on Sundays, but I can be there in about half an hour." I was relieved that he was coming, but I was also mindful of the economic implications of his offer to help.

Bob arrived in his glistening red wrecker, and we drove to the campground. As I got out of the tow truck, I turned around and watched in utter amazement as Bob leveraged himself out of the truck on braces and crutches. He was a paraplegic!

He made his way over to the camper, and I again began the mental gymnastics of calculating the cost of his beneficence.

"Yep, it's just a dead battery. A little jump start and you'll be on your way." Bob restored the battery, and while it was recharging, he entertained my daughter with magic tricks. He even pulled a quarter out of his ear and gave it to her.

As he was putting his jumper cables back into the truck, I asked him how much I owed him. "Oh, nothing," he replied, to my astonishment.

"I need to pay you something," I insisted.

"No," he reiterated. "Back in Vietnam, someone helped

me out of a worse situation than this when I lost my legs, and that guy told me to just pass it on. So you don't owe me anything. Just remember, whenever you get the chance, you pass it on."

Fast-forward about 20 years to my busy medical office, where I frequently train medical students. Cindy, a second-year student from an out-of-state school, has come to spend a month with me so that she can stay with her mother, who lives in the area. We have just finished seeing a patient whose life has been ravaged by drug and alcohol abuse. Cindy and I are in the nurses' station discussing possible treatment options, and suddenly I notice tears welling up in her eyes. "Are you uncomfortable talking about this sort of thing?" I asked.

"No," Cindy sobbed. "It's just that my mother could be that patient. She has the same problem."

We spent the lunch hour secluded in the conference room, discussing the tragic history of Cindy's alcoholic mom. Tearfully and painfully, Cindy bared her soul as she recounted the years of anger, embarrassment and hostility that had characterized her family's existence. I offered Cindy the hope of getting her mother into treatment, and we arranged for her mom to meet with a trained counselor. After strong encouragement from the other family members, Cindy's mom readily consented to treatment. She went into the hospital for several weeks and emerged a new and changed person. Cindy's family had been on the verge of disintegration; for the first time, they experienced a glimmer of hope. "How can I ever repay you?" Cindy asked.

As I thought back to that comatose camper in the snowbound campground and the paraplegic good Samaritan, I knew there was only one answer I could give her. "Just pass it on."

Kenneth G. Davis, M.D.

Wednesday Mornings with Elvis

A person who sows seeds of kindness enjoys a perpetual harvest.

Anonymous

I have worked as a cleaning lady for 14 years. One of my favorite customers of all time was old Mrs. Avadesian. She was wiry, like a spring, and seemed to bounce constantly, her white bun flying this way and that. I'm not sure how old she was, but I do know she buried the last of her six children a few years ago, all of whom had been on Social Security for some time. I knew something else about Mrs. Avadesian that no one in her family, not even her six children or any of her friends, ever knew. It was our little secret.

Mrs. Avadesian was crazy about Elvis.

That discovery came quite by surprise one morning when I caught her hiding something behind her back as I walked into the living room.

"Oh, my!" she stammered, backing away. We stood facing each other for what seemed like a long time. Her eyes looked this way and that, then tentatively into mine, testing my loyalty and searching for camaraderie. She found it and her face lit up.

She decided to share her special secret with me. Out came the secret in living color—that is, in faded living color: Elvis himself, smiling up at us both from a 1956 *Teen Magazine* with that "I am the King and I am one smokin' dude" grin. I looked up at Mrs. Avadesian. Her face was flushed.

Every Wednesday after that, the King came to Mrs. Avadesian's house for a personal visit. At exactly 9 A.M., I'd haul my cleaning stuff over to her tottering Victorian home and there'd she be, pacing nervously back and forth near the front window. She'd be dressed to the nines in her white appliquéd organza wedding dress, a single strand of tinted pearls and pink satin slippers.

It was also the morning her hair came down. Pin by pin she would loosen her bun, until silky silver tendrils drifted down, framing her face. Her face was an explosion of color against old bleached canvas: pearly pink, iridescent lips, magenta eye shadow placed in the general vicinity of her lids and tomato-red cheeks.

She'd wait in the parlor and then, my cleaning done, I'd march right over to the old Victrola, reach into my cleaning bag and pull out our new treasure—a somewhat scratchy but perfectly usable copy of "Elvis' Greatest Hits" that I fought for and won at a yard sale. I'd walk over to Mrs. Avadesian, take her tiny hand, bow and lead her onto the dance floor. After a measure or two, Elvis would join us from the Victrola in the corner, and there on the beat of three, we would all get crazy.

There was Elvis beboppin' about his "burnin' love," and Mrs. Avadesian and her white organza wedding dress, flapping and flipping and tripping everywhere but loose, her pink satin slippers burning up the rug.

We were "all shook up," yelling and yelping and jumping up and down. When we thought we couldn't take it for one more minute, Elvis turned up the pace with "Jailhouse Rock." He was relentless. He exhausted us. We begged him, "Please, Elvis, 'don't be cruel.'"

For the grand finale, Elvis serenaded us and swore to us his undying love and devotion. That's when I'd swoop Mrs. Avadesian up in my arms and waltz her across the floor. We took turns leading as our man crooned "Love Me Tender."

And he did. Every Wednesday morning, for all the Wednesdays Mrs. Avadesian had left.

Joy Curci

Holy Cow

In 1978, my car needed some mechanical work that I could not do myself. Since the garage I had been taking my car to had closed, I was faced with the daunting task of finding a good, honest mechanic. I was worried, given the—perhaps undeserved—reputations of mechanics as rip-off artists. Luckily, my friend Dave gave me a recommendation: D's Auto Repair.

I was pleasantly surprised to discover that the owner of D's was a mechanic who had worked on my car several years earlier. Back then, he was an employee at a gas station near my house. I never really spoke to him that much before, but I knew that his work was good.

I filled out the paperwork for the repair and waited while D took a phone call from another customer. As I sat there, I looked around the small office to keep myself occupied. A framed newspaper article caught my attention. The headline read: "Local Dairy Farmer Kills Whole Herd." The article was about the actions of a fifth-generation dairy farmer during the tainted milk scare in Michigan several years earlier. Apparently, dairy cows were becoming infected with a disease that was affecting the milk supply. The situation had become serious enough that the state decided to test all the cows in Michigan for the disease. The dairy lobby protested and the state was issued a restraining order. It appeared as though it would take months of legal jockeying before the dilemma could be resolved. In the meantime, dairy farmers could continue to sell milk, and also their cows for beef.

The fifth-generation dairy farmer decided this plan wouldn't work for him and chose another avenue. He paid to have all of his cows tested. Out of the entire herd, only a few were found to be infected. Because no one could assure that the other cows were totally safe, he had the herd killed and buried in a way that would not harm the environment or the water supply. The farmer's insurance did not cover the loss because the state had not issued an order for him to dispose of the herd. Asked why he did it, the farmer replied, "Because it was the right thing to do."

I asked D why he displayed the article on the wall. I thought that he might be related to or somehow knew the farmer. He said he had never met the man, but that the farmer was an inspiration to him and set a standard for integrity, trust and honesty. He said that is how he operated his auto repair business and that he would like to have people say the same kind of things about him that he said about the farmer.

I was now doubly impressed, with both the farmer and with D. The next year, on my recommendation, my son started a nine-month mechanics apprenticeship at D's Auto Repair. I wanted my son to study with D, not only because he was a good mechanic, but more importantly because he was an honest man of high integrity. May the same be said of me someday.

Dennis J. McCauley
Submitted by Charmian Anderson, Ph.D.

A Million-Dollar Lesson

*All labor that uplifts humanity has dignity
and importance and should be undertaken with
painstaking excellence.*

Martin Luther King Jr.

I had flown into Dallas for the sole purpose of calling on
one client. Time was of the essence, and my plan included
a quick turnaround trip from and back to the airport. A
spotless cab pulled up. The driver rushed to open the passenger door for me and made sure I was comfortably
seated before he closed it. As he got into the driver's seat,
he mentioned that the neatly folded *Wall Street Journal* next
to me was for my use. He then showed me several tapes
and asked me what type of music I would enjoy. Well! I
looked around to see if I was on *Candid Camera*. Wouldn't
you? I could not believe the service I was receiving.
"Obviously you take great pride in your work," I said to
the driver. "You must have a story to tell."

He did. "I used to be in Corporate America," he began.
"But I got tired of thinking my best would never be good

enough, fast enough, or appreciated enough. I decided to find my niche in life where I could feel proud of being the best I could be. I knew I would never be a rocket scientist, but I love driving cars, being of service, and feeling like I have done a full day's work and done it well."

After evaluating his personal assets, he decided to become a cab driver. "Not just a regular taxi hack," he continued, "but a professional cab driver. One thing I know for sure, to be good in my business I could simply just meet the expectations of my passengers. But to be *great* in my business, I'd have to *exceed* the customer's expectations. I like the sound of being 'great' better than just getting by on 'average.'"

Did I tip him big time? You bet. Corporate America's loss is the traveling folks' gain!

Petey Parker

Speak the Customer's Language

Example is not the main thing in influencing others. It is the only *thing.*

Albert Schweitzer

In 1955, when I was office head salesman in Procter & Gamble's Memphis district, I was assigned to spend a day in the field with the district's senior sales rep, Charlie "Soapy" Asbury. Charlie had been around for over 20 years and was a legend in Mississippi, where he had always lived and worked. It seemed like virtually every retail store owner and retail clerk knew Soapy; these people would wait impatiently from month to month just to hear his tales, his jokes and, of course, his spiel lauding P&G's soaps. Young sales reps who were assigned to work with Soapy considered it an honor as well as an invaluable learning experience.

That day in the Mississippi Delta country was an eye-opener for me. To my surprise, Soapy did not use any of the proven techniques we had all been taught from the manual. He just walked in and took over a store by sheer force of personality. His arrival at any of these small mom-and-pop stores, which controlled the business in that area (there were no supermarkets in this territory in those days), was equivalent to a movie star making a grand entry. Everyone, including the customers, looked up to Charlie and treated him as somebody special.

One of my first stops with Charlie was at a very small store that was typical of the time and place. Out front was an antique gasoline pump; two hound dogs sat on the small porch. Waiting for Charlie inside were the Chinese couple who owned the store. They lived in a room just behind the selling area of this tiny store. And, as I quickly observed, their command of English was limited.

The first words out of Soapy's mouth were, "Is your bed soft or hard, Mr. Bing?"

Without a moment's hesitation, Mr. Bing replied, "Bed is hard!"

Hearing this, Soapy declared, "Thank you very much, Mr. Bing. I'll see you next trip."

As soon as we got outside, I asked Soapy what that had been all about. He explained that due to lack of storage space, Mr. Bing kept all the cases of his P & G products under his bed in the back room. Therefore, when the bed was hard, he had ample inventory; but when the bed was soft, he needed to reorder from Soapy.

Soapy knew everything about his customers.

Lou Pritchett

How to Keep Clients . . . Even When It Hurts

Only those who risk going too far can possibly find out how far one can go.

T.S. Eliot

There is nothing more important to the success of a business than satisfied clients. Satisfied clients stay with you and refer their friends to you. Plus, keeping an existing client costs you a fraction of what it takes to bring in a new client to replace a dissatisfied one that has left. The single biggest reason clients leave is broken promises. The single most important rule for keeping your clients is: "When you make a promise, either stated or implied, do your best to keep it, regardless of the cost."

I was home in Columbus, Ohio, sound asleep. It was 2 A.M., and I was awakened by a phone call: one of my clients. I was scheduled to give a presentation in Marco Island, Florida, later that same morning at 9 A.M., and I was supposed to have arrived the night before. Panic set in. For some reason, I thought the program was in two days.

How did this happen? It didn't matter. The immediate problem was a speech that had to be done in seven hours, and I was a thousand miles away with no conceivable way to get there.

I frantically started looking through the Yellow Pages for charter planes. I called six or seven, but no one was answering at two in the morning. Finally one did. It was an air ambulance service. The guy asked me what the emergency was. I told him that if I wasn't in Marco Island by 7 A.M. that morning, my client was going to kill me. I asked if they could do it. He responded by asking me if I had an American Express card. As I quoted my Corporate Card number over the phone, he assured me there was no problem. Their Lear jet ambulance would have me there by 7 A.M.

I called the client back and told him that I had chartered, at my own expense, a Lear jet and would be there by 7 A.M. I heard a sigh of relief as he told me he would have a driver waiting for me at the Marco Island airport. At about 3 A.M., I rushed to the office to get my stuff, grabbed a two-liter bottle of diet soda, and ran off to await the arrival of my air ambulance. While I waited, I drank the two-liter bottle of soda.

About 40 minutes into the flight, the two liters of diet soda were ready to make an exit. I then discovered this Lear jet came with just about everything, including a registered nurse named Sandy. The only thing it didn't come with was a bathroom . . . and there was no way I could wait another 90 minutes. There were no bedpans, bottles or containers to help me out. Not to worry. Sandy's got the solution: catheterization. No way! I then asked the pilots what they did on long trips. One of them reached into his leather case, pulled out a plastic sandwich bag with one of those press-and-close tops, emptied out the carrot sticks and handed it to me while giving me a piece of very important advice. "When you seal it, make sure the yellow and blue stripes at the tip turn green."

The plane landed a little before eight. Just before I "de-Leared," the pilot asked me how long I was going to be. The speech was 45 minutes, with a book-signing afterward. I figured I'd be done about noon. "Great," he responded. "We'll wait." How about that? The return trip was free.

The limo got me to the hotel in plenty of time to clean up and prepare. I then gave one of the best presentations of my life. Everything clicked perfectly. Pure adrenaline.

The client was very impressed and appreciative that I was able to honor my commitment and that I was willing to do so, regardless of the cost. Oh yes . . . the cost. It was $7,000. Then to pour a little salt in the wound, they tacked on a 10-percent excise tax because it was a passenger ticket. Had I let Sandy catheterize me, I would have been a medical passenger and saved $700! And on top of that, there were no frequent flyer miles.

It was an adventure I won't soon forget, especially the bill. But the client was ecstatic, and I've received a lot of spin-off work and great word-of-mouth exposure—not to mention a great personal example to share in my speeches. Keeping the client's needs first always pays . . even when it costs.

Jeff Slutsky

Have You Received
Our Letter Yet?

A colleague, Pat Townsend, reported an example of Perdue Farms' response to a customer (remember, this is a three-quarter-*billion*-dollar company):

"A friend of mine mentioned last week that he once bought a Perdue chicken that, he discovered after getting home, was all dry and nasty. He took it back to the store and got an immediate refund. Then he decided to write Frank—having seen him on TV—and tell him that he had bought one of his damn quality chickens and it was all dry and nasty.

"By return mail he got a letter from Frank that not only included profuse apologies and a certificate for a free chicken, but that also enlisted his help to make sure it never happened again, by asking a whole list of specific questions: Where did he buy it? When? Exactly what was wrong? What did he think had happened? What exactly did the store say when he returned it? Et cetera, et cetera. Two days later an executive of Perdue Chickens *called* to make sure he'd received the letter, to make sure that all was well, and to ask some more specific questions. My friend will never buy anything but Perdue chicken."

Tom Peters

Someone Was Listening

The ability to accept responsibility is the measure of the man.

Roy L. Smith

By the end of 1992, Tom's of Maine had entered successfully into new markets up and down the West Coast, from Seattle to San Diego, increased our share of old markets, and produced strong balance sheets across the board. In the meantime, we had introduced company-wide retirement savings and profit-sharing plans, child care benefits, and parental leave—all within a company doubling in sales size every three years. Our clear sense of identity and purpose had helped us flourish financially.

We ended up having an expensive problem with our deodorant. Eager to improve our Honeysuckle Deodorant, we added lichen to the existing coriander, both of which are natural antimicrobials, thus doubling the deodorant's odor-eating power. Because of our corporate goal of decreasing our dependence on petroleum, we replaced a petroleum derivative in the deodorant (propylene glycol) with a vegetable-based glycerin. After a favorable response in tests among an in-house group, we put the new reformulation on the shelves.

Within two months the first complaints began, then increased exponentially over the next several weeks. Scores of angry customers were on the telephone to tell us that their deodorant was conking out halfway through the day. A quick series of consumer tests confirmed that half of our customers were pleased and half definitely were not. We went back to the lab and increased the amount of the lichen and coriander for better deodorant protection.

But the complaints didn't stop, and the heat from customers and stores soon demoralized the marketing and sales departments. We finally decided to put effectiveness before our principle of decreasing petroleum and replaced the glycerin with the propylene glycol. We sent samples to 200 of our angriest customers, and they loved it. Marketing and sales recommended a complete recall of the weak deodorant. To justify their decision, they pointed to our mission, which stated the company's aim "to serve our customers by providing safe, effective, innovative natural products of high quality." By that measure, the deodorant with the addition of the petroleum ingredient—the most effective product we had ever made— did not make the grade either.

A product recall would cost $400,000—a significant bite, to say the least, in our anticipated profits for the year. We had a genuine moral dilemma—profits versus values. I pointed out that our mission was not a one-sided document; it also calls on the company to respect the stockholders and all other financially interested parties. (I was not unaware of the irony—here was the values-oriented CEO reminding his marketing and sales department of the bottom line!) If we were to admit failure, we'd have to rein in plans in the works to crank up our successful ventures.

My managers agreed to slow down growth and reduce marketing investments that were already in the works, in order to assure a respectable profit for the year. It was a more cautious approach that placed profit goals before growth-rate goals, but it still protected the trust of our customers and the aspirations of our shareholders.

I authorized the $400,000 recall and thus said good-bye to 30 percent of our projected annual profits. It was a painful decision to make, but our sense of identity as a corporation committed to safety, effectiveness and trust as well as profits showed us the way out of the crisis. Our ideals won out. Our mission held up to the test of its central belief: The company can be financially successful, while behaving in a socially responsible and environmentally sensitive manner.

There was one catch: What to do with the old inventory? Depositing it in the dump would create a serious environmental problem. Colleen Myers came up with a happy solution. A national organization that worked with the homeless said it wanted the product—in spite of its marginal effectiveness—as part of its program to retrain people in personal hygiene habits.

But Tom's had disappointed thousands of loyal customers. We wrote to the 2,000 who had complained, explaining what had happened and apologizing. We gave them a free sample of the new formulation; 98 percent liked it and expressed their appreciation both for the new deodorant and for how the company had handled itself. Someone was listening.

Tom Chappell

Beyond Expectations

*Here is a simple but powerful rule: Always give
people more than they expect to get.*

Nelson Boswell

It seems a car dealership in my hometown of
Albuquerque was selling, on average, six to eight new cars
a day, six days a week. I was also told that 72 percent of
this dealership's first-time visitors returned for a second
visit. (At that time, the average for all dealerships in
Albuquerque for second-time visitors was 8 percent.)

I was curious and intrigued. How does a car dealership
get 72 percent of its first-time visitors to return? And how
can they sell six to eight cars a day in a slumping car
market?

When I walked into Saturn of Albuquerque that Friday
four years ago, the staff there didn't know me from Adam;
yet they shared with me their pricing policy, the profit
margin on every model, and staff income. They even
opened their training manuals for my review and invited
me back on Saturday if I wanted more information

(an invitation I heartily accepted).

I learned that this dealership (like all Saturn dealerships) has a "no-dicker sticker" policy; that is, the price on the window is the price you pay for the car. Period. You can't even negotiate for a free set of floor mats. Saturn abides by its premise of selling high-quality automobiles for a reasonable price.

Furthermore, Saturn sales consultants (their term for customer-contact people) aren't paid a commission—they're salaried. This means when you walk onto the showroom floor you're not bombarded with what I refer to as "beyond eager" sales people.

I expanded my research to other dealerships in Albuquerque. It turned out that Ford Escorts, LTDs and Thunderbirds, as well as the Mercury Marquis, were also sold as "no-dicker sticker" cars. As Bruce Sutherland at Richardson Ford said, "We were losing our market to Saturn because of their pricing and salary policies." He also said, "If we all did what Saturn was doing, we'd not only make a decent living, but we'd also enjoy a better reputation."

On Sunday, the day after my second visit to the Saturn store (their term, not mine), my wife, Jane, and I were walking as we frequently do. On this particular June morning, Jane gently slipped her hand in mine and said tenderly, "I don't know if you remember, but today's my fifth anniversary of being cancer-free." She was diagnosed with breast cancer five years ago and had undergone surgery. I was stunned, partially because I was embarrassed that I had forgotten, and, partially, because ... well, it seems we spend all of our time earning a living and never stop to live our earnings. I mean, isn't this what it's really all about?

I didn't know what to do with Jane's information. I spoke to her tenderly. All day. I took her to lunch. I bought the lunch. It was a nice, intimate day.

The next day, Monday, Jane went off to work teaching school. Still beside myself not knowing what to do to mark this special occasion, I did the most impetuous thing I've ever done in my life: I bought a new Saturn. I bought every accessory they produce in Springhill, Tennessee, to hang on that car. There wasn't an accessory made that I didn't buy. I didn't pick the color and I didn't pick the model, but I paid cash and told them I'd bring Jane in on Wednesday at 4:30 to make those two decisions. I told them why I was buying the car, and that it was my secret and they were not to reveal anything to her.

Tuesday morning, it dawned on me that Jane always wanted a white car. I called our sales consultant at Saturn, and I asked him if he had anything white in the store. He said he had one left but he couldn't guarantee it'd still be available Wednesday at 4:30 because they were selling so fast. I said I'd take my chances and asked him to put it in the showroom.

Wednesday came and went. Unexpectedly, someone in our family was admitted to the hospital. So, it wasn't until 9:30 Saturday morning when, after telling Jane the biggest lie to get her out of the house, we finally made our way to the Saturn store. I quickly turned into the parking lot and Jane angrily asked, "What are you doing? You promised me we'd get home right away." I said, "I'm sorry, I forgot I have to pick up something here for my Kiwanis speech next week."

Jane had never been in a Saturn store. When we went through the front door, the Lord took control of her feet and her mouth. She saw that little white Saturn coupe all the way across the showroom floor. She quickly passed a multi-colored sea of automobiles, sat in the little white Saturn and said, "Oh, what a pretty little car. Can I have a new car?" I said, "No. Not until Charlie graduates from college." Our son, Charlie, was attending the University of

New South Wales in Sydney, Australia (we call that "out of state" tuition). She said, "I'm sick and tired of driving that old Dodge, I want a new car." I said, "I promise, just three more semesters and he'll be out."

Next, Jane walked around to the front of the car. As she looked it over, she let out the most blood-curdling, shrill scream I'd ever heard in 29 years of marriage.

Now, before I tell you why Jane screamed, let me tell you what our sales consultant had done. He had ordered a large, professionally engraved sign (white letters on blue) and affixed the Saturn company logo on it. The sign stood alone on the hood of the little white Saturn coupe. It said:

> *Congratulations, Jane. This car is yours. Five years cancer-free. Let's celebrate life. From Milt, Billy and Team Saturn*

Every employee at Saturn of Albuquerque had endorsed the back of that sign. Jane saw it, screamed, collapsed in my arms and bawled her eyes out. I didn't know what to do. I was in tears. I took out my invoice from the previous Monday, unfolded it and, pointing to the white coupe, said, "No, honey, this car isn't yours. I bought you *this* one." I tapped the invoice with my index finger. Jane said, "No, I want this one right here." Charlie, who was home from college and with us, said, "No, Mom. Dad bought you anything you want in Springhill, Tennessee, or anything on the lot here." Jane said, "You don't understand, I want this one."

While this conversation was going on, I looked around and discovered that there was no one in the store. Our sales consultant had arranged it so that we could share the moment alone. The mechanics, the clerical staff, the front-desk receptionist, management and all sales consultants had left the store for the sanctity of our event.

Even so, it's impossible to have a lot of privacy when so many people are standing outside the showroom windows looking in. When Jane screamed and collapsed in my arms, I saw everybody outside applaud and begin to cry. Every new customer that came to the store in those minutes was not allowed to enter; instead, the staff took them aside and explained what was happening.

Jane never drove the car until she took it through the showroom door that day to drive it home.

Over the years, I've told this story in the United States, Australia and Indonesia as an example of legendary service. A woman in my audience in San Francisco from Anchorage, Alaska, heard the story; she called Saturn of Albuquerque long distance and bought a new car. It's like Ken Blanchard says, "It's only the stories told about us that differentiate us in the market place."

Milt Garrett
Submitted by Ken Blanchard

BIZARRO

By DAN PIRARO

The "Bizarro" cartoon by Dan Piraro is reprinted courtesy Chronicle Features, San Francisco, California.

5

FOLLOW
YOUR HEART

*Your work is to discover your work, and then
with all your heart to give yourself to it.*

Buddha

To Have Succeeded

To laugh often and love much;
To win the respect of intelligent people
And the affection of children;
To earn the approbation of honest critics
And endure the betrayal of false friends;
To appreciate beauty;
To find the best in others;
To give one's self;
To leave the world a little better,
Whether by a healthy child,
A garden patch,
Or a redeemed social condition;
To have played and laughed with enthusiasm
And sung with exultation;
To know even one life has breathed easier
Because you have lived . . .
This is to have succeeded.

Ralph Waldo Emerson

Making Bright Memories
for Tomorrow

I don't know what your destiny will be, but one thing I know: The only ones among you who will be truly happy are those who will have sought and found how to serve.

Albert Schweitzer

People who have known me for a long time refuse to believe that I work in a nursing facility. Certainly they would not believe how much I love my job.

They are unwilling to let me forget the years our Sunday school class held a weekly service in a nursing facility. I was always the last to volunteer. Those who have known me longest also remember when I had little patience with an elderly neighbor. I was the one who labeled all senior citizens "boring."

That was before I met Miss Lilly. Miss Lilly changed a lot of things in my life. Since meeting her, I'll never feel the same about the older generation, about nursing facilities, or even about life.

I had heard many negative remarks about our local nursing facility and admit I applied for a job there only because it was close to my home—thinking to myself, I could always quit. Yes, the receptionist assured me when I went to apply, they did need a nurse's aide. "Are you certified?"

"Not yet," I answered, wondering how in the world one got certified. Application in hand, I was directed to a sunny room. I seated myself at a table facing two dozen or more elderly ladies. They were being led in exercise by an unsmiling woman, clad in black pants and a drab, gray blouse. Her voice was a monotone. She had about the same amount of enthusiasm a gunfighter might muster up for his own hanging. I wondered what her job was. Just as I started to write "nurse's aide" in the blank that read "position applied for," she read aloud from a letter. "Dear Activity Director," she read. So that's what she was. I wrote "activity director" in the blank instead. I knew I could do a better job than that sourpuss. I knew how to smile, and my wardrobe contained plenty of bright colors.

Unemployed, I had fallen into the bad habit of sleeping late. When the shrill ringing of the telephone woke me, it was 8:05 A.M. The woman on the other end sounded cheerful and confident. "I have your application for activity director," she said. "We are about to open a new unit. What are your qualifications?"

Trying my best to sound awake, I answered, "I used to teach school." I failed to mention it was elementary school and 20 years ago.

"How soon can you be here?" she asked.

I sat up straight in bed. "One hour. I can come in one hour."

From that day on, my life changed. It is no longer mine alone. Each waking moment my thoughts are on the residents. Is Billie all right? How is Mr. W? Will Janie be back from the hospital today?

The residents fill my thoughts and they fill my heart—these lonely, fragile people who all have a story to tell and love to give. I have yet to meet one who is "boring."

My first love was Miss Lilly, a lonely woman with only one living relative. Miss Lilly was not a pretty sight. She was a broad-shouldered woman with large hands and feet, in a near prone position. She spent her days in a blue geri chair. She drooled constantly, her large mouth often hanging open to expose several stained, broken teeth in blood-red gums. Her hair, sparse and iron-gray, had twin cowlicks that caused it to stick out in all directions. Worse yet, Miss Lilly never spoke.

I had seen her one relative, a niece, several times. Each visit was the same. Standing a few feet in front of the blue chair she would say, "Your check came, your bill is paid." Never a personal word, a hug, or any sign of affection.

Was it any wonder Miss Lilly had retreated from what must have seemed a cruel, uncaring world? Months passed, and Miss Lilly seemed to shrink lower and lower down in her chair. Plainly, her health was deteriorating. I was staying longer and longer in her unit. I discovered she was not eating well. I gave up my lunch hour to feed her. Seeing how much she enjoyed Jell-O and pudding, I brought her extra. I talked to her constantly—about the weather, current events, anything I could think of. Sometimes I held her hand. One day, to my amazement, she spoke. "Bend down," she said. Quickly I knelt at her side. "Put your arms around me and pretend you love me," she whispered. Me love Miss Lilly! I had never thought about it. I gathered her into my arms and felt my heart near bursting with love.

There have been many Miss Lillys in my life since then and I know there will be others. They are the ones who need more than kindness and care; they need a little piece of your heart. I love each day of work, sharing with the residents my life, my grandchildren, my joys and sorrows. They share with me their past, their fear of the future, their families, and most of all, their love.

My wardrobe encompasses a rainbow of colors. I have dressed as everything from a clown to an Easter bunny. Pink flamingos and speckled trout have dangled from my ears. The residents love it.

I now define nursing facilities as fun houses for mature persons. They are wonderful, caring places where witty, fun-loving seniors enjoy companionship.

My mission is to use each day of their lives to make a bright memory for tomorrow. We enjoy singing, laughing and playing games as if today were all we had. Sometimes it is. I wrote these lines soon after the death of Miss Lilly:

> *I touched her hand and spoke her name,*
> *the tired eyes opened wide.*
> *I looked and saw within their depths*
> *the loneliness inside.*
> *I clasped her fragile hand in mine,*
> *my warmth took off its chill.*
> *The love she put inside my heart*
> *I share with others still.*

Joyce Ayer Brown

I Found Myself Saying Yes

I am only one; but still I am one. I cannot do everything, but still I can do something. I will not refuse to do the something I can do.

Helen Keller

It was a normal spring day in 1950. I was asked to attend a meeting with the president of the medical school where I was an attending physician. He didn't tell me the purpose of the meeting, and when I arrived at his office, I was surprised to find five couples sitting with him. I sat down and wondered what these people had in common.

What they had in common was a problem: All were parents of retarded children, and nowhere in the vast city of New York were they able to find medical facilities to treat their children's special needs.

As they told me their story, I was shocked to learn how they had been mistreated, badly advised and humiliated; all because their children were retarded and did not "deserve" to be treated as other human beings with medical problems. They had been turned away from all the other teaching hospitals. Their request was simple: They were asking for a weekly clinic to treat the medical problems of the retarded.

Their stories touched me deeply and I felt embarrassed that this attitude existed among my medical colleagues. I soon found myself saying that I would set up a one-morning-a-week clinic for these children and their parents.

Little did I realize then that this decision was the beginning of a new life for me. I soon became the leader of the first and only facility of its kind in the world, tending to the physical needs of mentally retarded children. Parents with their children came out of the woodwork seeking help. I was completely overwhelmed, trying to attend to everyone's needs in just one morning a week. What should I do? I agonized over the decision of whether to devote my entire professional life to this mission, or to walk away. Needless to say, I decided to commit myself to the plight of this lonely community.

The unexpected spring meeting with those five couples led me to become an advocate, clinician, researcher, administrator and policy-maker. The five couples went on to found the National Association for Retarded Citizens. Jimmy Carter, then the president of the United States, appointed me the first director of the National Institute of Handicapped Research.

I had been challenged to reach deeply within myself to make a better life for all these individuals. I said yes . . . and I found my life's mission.

Margaret J. Giannini, M.D.

The Shadowland of Dreams

You are what your deep driving desire is,
As your desire is, so is your will.
As your will is, so is your deed.
As your deed is, so is your destiny.

Brihadaranyaka Upanishad IV.4.5

Many a young person tells me he wants to be a writer. I always encourage such people, but I also explain that there's a big difference between "being a writer" and writing. In most cases these individuals are dreaming of wealth and fame, not the long hours alone at the typewriter. "You've got to want to write," I say to them, "not want to be a writer."

The reality is that writing is a lonely, private and poor-paying affair. For every writer kissed by fortune, there are thousands more whose longing is never requited. Even those who succeed often know long periods of neglect and poverty. I did.

When I left a 20-year career in the Coast Guard to become a freelance writer, I had no prospects at all. What

I did have was a friend with whom I'd grown up in Henning, Tennessee. George found me my home—a cleaned-out storage room in the Greenwich Village apartment building where he worked as superintendent. It didn't even matter that it was cold and had no bathroom. Immediately I bought a used manual typewriter and felt like a genuine writer.

After a year or so, however, I still hadn't received a break and began to doubt myself. It was so hard to sell a story that I barely made enough to eat. But I knew I wanted to write. I had dreamed about it for years. I wasn't going to be one of those people who die wondering, "What if?" I would keep putting my dream to the test— even though it meant living with uncertainty and fear of failure. This is the Shadowland of hope, and anyone with a dream must learn to live there.

Then one day I got a call that changed my life. It wasn't an agent or editor offering a big contract. It was the opposite—a kind of siren call tempting me to give up my dream. On the phone was an old acquaintance from the Coast Guard, now stationed in San Francisco. He had once lent me a few bucks and liked to egg me about it. "When am I going to get the $15, Alex?" he teased.

"Next time I make a sale."

"I have a better idea," he said. "We need a new public-information assistant out here, and we're paying $6,000 a year. If you want it, you can have it."

Six thousand a year! That was real money in 1960. I could get a nice apartment, a used car, pay off debts and maybe save a little something. What's more, I could write on the side.

As the dollars were dancing in my head, something cleared my senses. From deep inside a bull-headed resolution welled up. I had dreamed of being a writer—full time. And that's what I was going to be. "Thanks, but no,"

I heard myself saying. "I'm going to stick it out and write."

Afterward, as I paced around my little room, I started to feel like a fool. Reaching into my cupboard—an orange crate nailed to the wall—I pulled out all that was there: two cans of sardines. Plunging my hands in my pockets, I came up with 18 cents. I took the cans and coins and jammed them into a crumpled paper bag. *There Alex*, I said to myself. *There's everything you've made of yourself so far.* I'm not sure I ever felt so low.

I wish I could say things started getting better right away. But they didn't. Thank goodness I had George to help me over the rough spots.

Through him I met other struggling artists, like Joe Delaney, a veteran painter from Knoxville, Tennessee. Often Joe lacked food money, so he'd visit a neighborhood butcher who would give him big bones with morsels of meat, and a grocer who would hand him some wilted vegetables. That's all Joe needed to make down-home soup.

Another Village neighbor was a handsome young singer who ran a struggling restaurant. Rumor had it that if a customer ordered steak, the singer would dash to a supermarket across the street to buy one. His name was Harry Belafonte.

People like Delaney and Belafonte became role models for me. I learned that you had to make sacrifices and live creatively to keep working at your dreams. That's what living in the Shadowland is all about.

As I absorbed the lesson, I gradually began to sell my articles. I was writing about what many people were talking about then: civil rights, black Americans and Africa. Soon, like birds flying south, my thoughts were drawn back to my childhood. In the silence of my room, I heard the voices of Grandma, Cousin Georgia, Aunt Plus, Aunt Liz and Aunt Till as they told stories about our family and slavery.

These were stories that black Americans had tended to avoid before, and so I mostly kept them to myself. But one day at lunch with editors of *Reader's Digest*, I told these stories of my grandmother and aunts and cousins. I said that I had a dream to trace my family's history to the first African brought to these shores in chains. I left that lunch with a contract that would help support my research and writing for nine years.

It was a long, slow climb out of the shadows. Yet in 1970, 17 years after I left the Coast Guard, *Roots* was published. Instantly I had the kind of fame and success that few writers ever experience. The shadows had turned into dazzling limelight.

For the first time I had money and open doors everywhere. The phone rang all the time with new friends and new deals. I packed up and moved to Los Angeles, where I could help in the making of the *Roots* TV mini-series. It was a confusing, exhilarating time, and in a sense, I was blinded by the light of my success.

Then one day, while unpacking, I came across a box filled with things I had owned years before in the Village. Inside was a brown paper bag.

I opened it, and there were two corroded sardine cans, a nickel, a dime and three pennies. Suddenly the past came flooding in like a riptide. I could picture myself once again huddled over the typewriter in that cold, bleak, one-room apartment. And I said to myself, *The things in this bag are part of my roots, too. I can't ever forget that.*

I sent them out to be framed in Lucite. I keep that clear plastic case where I can see it every day. I can see it now above my office desk in Knoxville, along with the Pulitzer Prize, a portrait of nine Emmys awarded to the TV production of *Roots*, and the Spingarn medal—the NAACP's highest honor. I'd be hard pressed to say which means the most to me. But only one reminds me of the courage and persistence it takes to stay the course in the Shadowland.

It's a lesson anyone with a dream should learn.

Alex Haley

I Never Write Right

There is a vitality, a life force, an energy, a quickening, that is translated through you into action, and because there is only one of you in all time, this expression is unique.

Martha Graham

When I was 15, I announced to my English class that I was going to write and illustrate my own books. Half the students sneered; the rest nearly fell out of their chairs laughing.

"Don't be silly. Only geniuses can become writers," the English teacher said smugly. "And you are getting a D this semester."

I was so humiliated I burst into tears. That night I wrote a short, sad poem about broken dreams and mailed it to the *Capper's Weekly* newspaper. To my astonishment they published it, and sent me two dollars. I was a published and paid writer! I showed my teacher and fellow students. They laughed.

"Just plain dumb luck," the teacher said.

I'd tasted success. I'd sold the first thing I'd ever written. That was more than any of them had done, and if it was "just dumb luck," that was fine with me.

During the next two years I sold dozens of poems, letters, jokes and recipes. By the time I graduated from high school (with a C-minus average), I had scrapbooks filled with my published work. I never mentioned my writing to my teachers, friends or my family again. They were dream killers, and if people must choose between their friends and their dreams, they must always choose their dreams.

But sometimes you do find a friend who supports your dreams. "It's easy to write a book," that new friend told me. "You can do it."

"I don't know if I'm smart enough," I said, suddenly feeling 15 again and hearing echoes of laughter.

"Nonsense!" she said. "Anyone can write a book if they want to."

I had four children at the time, and the oldest was only four. We lived on a goat farm in Oklahoma, miles from anyone. All I had to do each day was take care of four kids, milk goats, and do the cooking, laundry and gardening. No problem.

While the children napped, I typed on my ancient typewriter. I wrote what I felt. It took nine months, just like a baby.

I chose a publisher at random and put the manuscript in an empty Pampers diapers package, the only box I could find (I'd never heard of manuscript boxes). The letter I enclosed read: "I wrote this book myself, I hope you like it. I also drew the illustrations. Chapters 6 and 12 are my favorites. Thank you."

I tied a string around the diaper box and mailed it without a self-addressed stamped envelope, and without making a copy of the manuscript. A month later I received a contract, an advance on royalties and a request to start working on another book.

Crying Wind became a bestseller, was translated into 15 languages and Braille, and sold worldwide. I appeared on TV talk shows during the day and changed diapers at night. I traveled from New York to California and Canada on promotional tours. My first book also became required reading in Native American schools in Canada.

It took six months to write my next book. I mailed it in an empty Uncle Wiggley game box (I still hadn't heard of manuscript boxes). *My Searching Heart* also became a bestseller. I wrote my next novel, *When I Give My Heart,* in only three weeks.

The worst year I ever had as a writer, I earned two dollars (I was 15, remember?). In my best year, I earned $36,000. Most years I earn between $5,000 and $10,000. No, it isn't enough to live on, but it's still more than I'd make working part-time, and it's $5,000 to $10,000 more than I'd make if I didn't write at all.

People ask what college I attended, what degrees I have, and what qualifications I have to be a writer. The answer is none. I just write. I'm not a genius, I'm not gifted and I don't write right. I'm lazy, undisciplined, and spend more time with my children and friends than I do writing.

I didn't own a thesaurus until four years ago and I use a small Webster's dictionary that I bought at Kmart for 89 cents. I use an electric typewriter that I paid $129 for six years ago. I've never used a word processor. I do all the cooking, cleaning and laundry for a family of six and fit my writing in a few minutes here and there. I write everything in longhand on yellow tablets while sitting on the sofa with my four kids, eating pizza and watching TV. When the book is finished, I type it and mail it to the publisher.

I've written eight books. Four have been published, and three are still out with the publishers. One stinks.

To all those who dream of writing, I'm shouting at you, "Yes, you can! Yes, you can! Don't listen to them!" I don't write right, but I've beaten the odds. Writing is easy, it's fun, and anyone can do it. Of course, a little dumb luck doesn't hurt.

Linda Stafford

When Dreams Won't Die

Always bear in mind that your own resolution to succeed is more important than any other one thing.

Abraham Lincoln

Ever since I can remember, I've been fascinated by beauty. As a young girl surrounded by the numbing sameness of all those cornfields around Indianapolis, the glamorous worlds of fashion and cosmetics were a magnificent escape for me. Every time I looked at the advertisements in women's magazines—all those gorgeous models with flawless skin and expertly applied makeup, their statuesque bodies adorned with incredible designer outfits—I was whisked away to exotic places I could only revisit in dreams.

The Revlon ads were especially wonderful. But there was only one problem—not one ad in those days featured a woman of color like me. Still, there was a "whisper of wisdom" inside me, telling me that someday my dream would come true and I would have a career in the cosmetics industry.

Very few companies bothered to market cosmetics to women of color in those days, but my inspiration came from C. J. Walker, the first African-American woman to become a millionaire. She started out with two dollars and a dream, right in my own hometown. She earned the fortune at the turn of the century, with her own line of hair-care products just for women like herself.

I graduated from college with a degree in public health education. Before long I got a job with a leader in the pharmaceuticals industry—and became the first African-American woman to sell pharmaceuticals in Indiana. People were shocked that I took the job because a woman of color selling encyclopedias in my territory had just been killed. In fact, when I started, the physicians I dealt with looked at me as if I had two heads.

But eventually my uniqueness worked to my advantage. The doctors and nurses remembered me. And I reversed the negative halo effect by doing the job better than other people. Along with pharmaceuticals, I sold them Girl Scout cookies and helped the nurses with their makeup. They began to look forward to my coming, not just for the novelty, but because we enjoyed such heartwarming visits.

Within two years, I'd broken numerous sales records and was recognized as a Distinguished Sales Representative, formerly an all-white male club. I was looking forward to some hard-earned commission checks when suddenly, the company decided to subdivide the region and hired a handsome blond man to take my place. He would enjoy the fruits of my labor, while I was reassigned to another area that needed a lot of work. At this point, my dream of that cosmetics career with Revlon seemed a million miles away.

Discouraged and disenchanted, I picked up and moved to Los Angeles. Then one Sunday, as I searched longingly through the ads in the *Los Angeles Times,* there it was: a classified ad for a regional manager job with Revlon. I lit up completely and dove for the phone first thing Monday morning. The voice at the other end said that due to overwhelming response, Revlon was taking no more résumés.

I was devastated. But then a dear friend said to me, "Marilyn, I know you aren't going to let this job slip through your fingers. Go on down there anyway." Suddenly inspired and determined to turn the challenge into an adventure, I drove down to the Marriott where they were conducting interviews. When I arrived, a desk clerk curtly informed me that there was no way I could get an interview, nor would Mr. Rick English take my résumé. I walked away, smiling. At least I now had the name of the man I needed to see.

I decided to have lunch to listen for the whisper of wisdom that would provide me with a new strategy. Sure enough, the idea came to me to explain my situation to the cashier as I was about to leave the restaurant. She immediately picked up the phone to find out what room Mr. English was in. "Room 515," she said turning to me. My heart began to pound.

I stood outside room 515, said a prayer, and knocked on the door. The minute he opened the door I said, "You haven't met the best person for the job because you haven't talked to me yet."

He looked stunned and said, "Wait a minute until I finish this interview and I'll speak to you." When I entered the room, I was clear and firm that this job was for me, and I got the job.

My first day at Revlon was like a dream come true. They hired me to market a new line of hair-care products designed especially for people of color. And by the time I'd worked there three years, the public was beginning to demand natural, cruelty-free products.

With public sentiment on my side, here was my chance! Once again listening to the whisper of wisdom inside me, I opened my own cosmetics company, which to this day continues to give me a sense of fulfillment impossible to describe.

I truly believe we should never give up on our hopes and dreams. The path may be rocky and twisted, but the world is waiting for that special contribution each of us was born to make. What it takes is the courage to follow those whispers of wisdom that guide us from inside. When I listen to that, I expect nothing less than a miracle.

Marilyn Johnson Kondwani

Debbie Fields Gets "Oriented"

If a man write a better book, preach a better sermon, or make a better mouse-trap than his neighbor, tho' he build his house in the woods, the world will make a beaten path to his door.

Ralph Waldo Emerson

Debbie Fields is at a party with her husband, Randy Fields, a well-known economist and futurist. Debbie, just 19, has quit work to play the role of conventional wife, and her self-esteem is suffering. The guests fawn over Randy, soliciting his economic forecast. But when the same guests discover that Debbie is a housewife, they suddenly remember conversations they desperately need to have on the other side of the room. They treat Debbie like an absolute zero.

Finally, the host of the party besieges Debbie with questions. She tries hard to be what she really isn't— sophisticated, urbane, clever. Finally, he asks in an exasperated tone, "What do you intend to *do* with your life?"

By now a nervous wreck, Debbie blurts, "Well, I'm mostly trying to get orientated."

"The word is *oriented*," snaps the host. "There is no such word as *orientated*. Learn to use the English language."

Debbie is destroyed. On the way home, she cries nearly nonstop, but out of the hurt a resolve is born: She will never, never, *never* let such a thing happen again. She will no longer live in anyone else's shadow. She will find something of her own.

But what?

One thing Debbie had always loved doing was making great chocolate chip cookies. She experimented with recipes since she was 13 years old—adding more butter, less flour, more and different kinds of chocolate until she hit on a combination that she felt was ideal: soft, butter-laden, and crammed with so many chocolate chips that if one more were added, the whole cookie would collapse.

So Debbie has this idea. She will open up a little store and sell her cookies.

"Bad idea," Randy's business friends say, their mouths full of cookies. "It'll never work." They shake their heads as they lick the last bits of chocolate from their fingers. "Forget it." Randy felt the same way. So did the loan officers she approached for financing.

Notwithstanding, at 9 A.M. on August 18, 1977, when Debbie was 20 years old, she opened the doors to Mrs. Fields' Chocolate Chippery in nearby Palo Alto, California. The only problem was, nobody came to buy cookies. By noon she was desperate. "I decided if I were going to go out of business," she said, "at least I'd go out in style." So she loaded up a tray and began walking around the shopping arcade where her store was located, trying to give away cookies. "Nobody would take them," she said. Undaunted, she went out on the street and began begging, pleading and wheedling until people took her samples.

It worked. Once people tried the cookies, they loved them and came back to the shop for more. By the end of the day, she had sold $50 worth. On day two, she took in $75. The rest is cookie history.

"I owe my life to the word *oriented*," said Debbie.

Today, Debbie Fields is chairwoman and chief cookie lover of Mrs. Fields, Inc., the market leader among fresh-baked cookie stores. With over 600 stores and 1,000 corporate employees, Mrs. Fields Cookies has sales in the multi-millions. A mother of five, Debbie continues to share her winning philosophy with entrepreneurs and business groups around the world.

Celeste Fremon
from Moxie Magazine

A Walk in the "Woulds"

You never find yourself until you face the truth.

Pearl Bailey

I was doing well, running a district office in Denver for a Fortune 500 company. I had a company car, was making good money, was my own boss and could come and go as I pleased.

And I was bored. I was discovering the stress associated with doing something that neither held my attention nor gave me pleasure. I found myself getting into the office by 10:00 A.M. to avoid the rush hour traffic, and leaving by 4:00 P.M. to beat the traffic home. Subtract two hours for lunch, an hour for whatever, and I was working three hours a day.

My wife suggested that I go back to school to get a graduate degree. I took her advice, and my future was forever changed.

I was well-schooled in the world of business, comfortable with a spreadsheet and calculator. But because I had found people so different and so unpredictable, I'd stopped worrying about the people involved in a project with me and focused on just moving forward. Enter Leonard Chusmir, a former executive with Knight-Ridder and a formidable instructor. Leonard taught me that people do matter. He taught me to look behind the drama in people's lives. He helped me to see better the "why" in what people do or don't do. The power of his teaching lay not in the ability to analyze others, but in the ability to analyze myself.

Then I met a fellow night-scholar named Bruce Fitch. He ran the Professional Development Program for the Colorado Outward Bound School, and he asked me to participate in an upcoming program. He had a "Rolex" group coming in—senior executives making lots of money. Bruce felt my business background would help supplement the staff's professional background in mountaineering.

So there I was with a group of "go-getter" executives and managers from a Fortune 500 organization. We're out in some of the most beautiful land in the world. We're hiking, we're climbing, we are having the time of our lives.

I became friends with the group's senior ranking executive. "Would you like to go for a walk?" he asked me one night. We walked through the clear, star-filled night with the full moon as our guide. I was as content as a person can be, when suddenly, this senior executive started to cry. Then his shoulders started to heave and he appeared to be unraveling. I was schooled in business, not the human heart. We were miles from base camp and I was at a loss as to what to do.

After a while he began to speak of a life lived with no relationship with his wife, his children, or even with himself. "Do you want to know what a day in my life is like?" he asked. "When I finally get home, I have two or three martinis and fall asleep in front of the television, only to wake up and start over the next day. I've been dead from the neck down for as long as I can remember. For the first time, on this trip, I feel alive." And then he thanked me. I realized that this man's awakening to the poverty of his life was what my experiences, friends and wife had been telling me.

With that insight, I sat at the crossroads between *could* and *would*. I could continue to live my life as I had been, or I could choose a life that *would* make a difference in some-one's life, such as this man's.

Today, I only work with clients on what they would like to do, not on what they could do. I invite everyone to take a walk in the "woulds."

Jeff Hoye

A Sign for Our Times

*K*nowing *God's own time is best,*
In patient hope I rest . . .

John Greenleaf Whittier

One morning in 1975 in Greenwood, South Carolina, Dorothy Nicholas sat scribbling at her kitchen table. She was trying to compose an appropriate slogan. Even though Dorothy is an award-winning writer and former advertising copywriter, she sometimes has trouble finding just the right words. And she sensed that these needed to be perfect.

The words were for a sign hanging over the self-service gas station Dorothy managed with help from her disabled husband, Fred. They had started working a week ago, pulling their trailer from Orlando up to Greenwood, and the job seemed simple enough, just sitting at a drive-up window, taking money from customers.

"It was a bit of a lark," Dorothy admits. "Fred and I called a lot of places 'home' during those years because we both yearned to travel, and with our children grown, we could do it." Sometimes they settled for a while and took jobs, and this was one of those times.

There was already a lighted advertising sign on top of the building, but Dorothy's new boss had told her she could replace the message with anything she liked. "I had heard that this chain of stations was frequently robbed," Dorothy says, "so I was thinking about a safety-related slogan." At the same time, she felt that God was nudging her, encouraging her to make her trust in Him known to others. She tried several ideas, then inspiration struck.

"What do you think of this?" she asked Fred.

He studied her scrawl: *God Is Our Security Guard—Always on the Job.* "That says it pretty well," he told her. The next day, he spelled it out on the lighted board.

The sign was impressive, but it seemed to have little or no effect on anyone. Few customers commented on it.

After five months, the wanderlust struck again, and Dorothy and Fred resigned and took off in the trailer. Time passed. "Sometimes we would travel that route, going from Florida to South Carolina, and I always felt a little glow as we'd drive by the sign," Dorothy says. Subsequent managers had liked it well enough to keep it up. But remembering her strange urgency to find just the right words, Dorothy wondered if the sign had really mattered to God after all.

In 1988, Dorothy and Fred found themselves in Gainesville, Florida. At church they met Janet and Larry, a young couple living nearby. The four got along well, and when Dorothy and Fred had some temporary health problems, their new friends proved to be a blessing: running errands, providing an occasional meal, and just being there. "I don't know what we would have done without you," Dorothy told Larry more than once. She was growing quite fond of this kind, clean-cut young man.

One evening Dorothy invited Janet and Larry over for dinner. The four sat around the table, talking leisurely.

Fred and Dorothy were surprised to hear that Larry had grown up in Greenwood.

"Why, we worked there once—" Dorothy began. Had they ever met Larry? She started to ask him, but having begun to talk about himself, Larry couldn't stop.

"I've had a pretty rough past," he went on, pent-up words suddenly tumbling out. At 16, he'd become involved with the wrong crowd and had spent a year in reform school. After his release, he'd wanted to start over again, but because of his record, he couldn't find a job.

"One night in 1975," Larry continued, "I decided to rob a gas station for money to leave home." There was a self-service station nearby, so he stole his father's gun and car, and just before closing time, he drove up to rob the woman sitting at the window.

But before pulling his gun, he glanced at the roof of the building. There had always been a sign there, but someone had recently changed the words. "When I read the message," Larry said, "I knew I couldn't rob that place—or do anything else illegal." He went home, prayed all night and begged God to help him straighten out his life.

Dorothy and Fred looked at each other. "What did the sign say, Larry?" she asked gently.

"I've never forgotten those words," the young man assured her. "It said, 'God Is Our Security Guard—Always on the Job.' And He is, Dorothy. He guarded me from danger that night, and He has ever since."

Dorothy's heart lifted. It had taken 13 years, but now she knew the source of that strange longing, the need to find just the perfect words. For God had used her small act of faith to bring a lost child safely to His side.

Joan Wester Anderson

The names that appear in this story have been changed to protect the privacy of the actual individuals.

Sacred Stalls

No matter how deep a study you make, what you really have to rely on is your own intuition and when it comes down to it, you really don't know what's going to happen until you do it.

Konosuke Matsushita

We were a company that brokered highly trained technical human resources. My boss, Angela, and I were to fly to the East Coast to negotiate the renewal of a two-year, $26 million contract with our largest client. It was going to be a memorable day any way you cut it because as the account rep, I stood to either keep my job for the next two years or face the grueling task of finding another one.

I had had several conversations in the previous weeks with the client in which they had tried to cushion us for the fall by saying that not only could they *not* pay the increase we were asking of them, but that we should voluntarily reduce our fees. My boss had made it clear to them that she had no intentions of backing off from her fee increase. In our private meeting, she had told me that the thing for us to do was to prepare a slide presentation to justify the fee increase.

I was never totally comfortable with this idea because I remembered how strong the client was about needing a fee reduction in order to stay in business with us at all. I feared we could easily end up $26 million poorer.

I tried to diplomatically discuss these fears with my boss, but she was determined. She decided to "make them kowtow" to her for once, instead of the other way around. The picture that came to mind was of a shoot-out in the old corral—you know, the kind with a lot of bloodshed and orphaned children.

We met in a beautiful, mahogany-appointed board-room. Angela gave the slide presentation, and then she seated herself beside me and across the wide table from the three top managers. I inwardly cringed at the obvious "us and them" seating arrangement.

After 30 minutes of some uncomfortable, "blame-you, defend-me" and then patronizing "blame-me, defend-you" language from both sides, Angela started to cry. I couldn't believe it! Now what? They apologized, saying it was not their intention to hurt her feelings, but that they had to stand firm in the interest of the future of their company. I could see that they felt manipulated by the tears and were being polite. I could also see we were in the toilet on this one, and that I might be looking for another job real soon.

I asked if we could take a five-minute break. They all thought that was a good idea. Then I asked Angela if she would come with me to the ladies' room.

Once in the ladies' room, I asked Angela if I could try something. She said, "Okay, at this point, I don't think you could do any harm anyway. I'm going outside for some air." I was thankful for the privacy of a bathroom stall at that moment because I had no clue how to save the day. I put my head in my hands and I prayed. A very

wise teacher once said that prayer is simply consciousness asking itself for help. After many years of thinking
prayer was for babies, I had given myself permission to
pray again. It was such a relief.

I took some deep breaths and allowed my mind to imagine the entire scene ahead of me as I would like it to play
out. What I saw was the three of them and the two of us sitting in a circle with our hearts showing through our
clothes, beating bright red. I knew in that moment that I
needed to keep my awareness on my heart, no matter what
else. Then I saw them laughing. The thought of laughter
caused me to relax, although I couldn't imagine what
would cause us to laugh like that. Somehow, I felt okay
about returning to the group. And I noticed that I could be
okay with whatever the outcome might turn out to be.

When we reconvened, I talked about a few loose, mun-
dane business details that needed some discussion. At
one point, I slipped and said *porpoise* instead of *purpose* and
we all laughed. It was the thing that broke the ice. For a
few minutes we were all just human beings having a
laugh. The slip caused me to remember that one of our
consultants had recently been invited by one of the
client's largest customers on a family outing at Sea World.
The older couple owned a lab that our consultant had
helped design. They had grown close, frequently invited
her for dinner and eventually adopted her as the daughter they'd never had. The client was very interested in
this story. I mentioned that this was only one of the multitude of stories of how our consultants were having a
great life on the road, developing community around the
country with their customers.

After a few minutes of more stories, I noticed how the
energy in the room had softened. At that moment, we
were simply reflecting on the good times, and everyone in
the room was enjoying themselves.

Then I laughed and said, "You didn't know you were financing community and 'family' reunions, did you?"

The vice president said, "Marty, if sponsoring family reunions gets me more business, then I'm in the business of sponsoring family reunions. Why don't you go back to your office and work up the numbers for me. If you can prove that replacing your stellar team of consultants would cost us more in the long run, I'll sign this contract at your present rates. How's that for a good compromise?"

It felt like a miracle had just happened. And what's even more amazing is that when Angela and I had a debriefing session about the trip, I was offered a promotion to vice president—and a raise, to boot!

Marty Raphael

A Hug from a Teenage Boy

No act of kindness, no matter how small, is ever wasted.

Aesop

Fifteen years spent in the field of education have provided me with many treasured moments. One of the most endearing happened when I was teaching second grade, 10 years ago.

In May of the fourth quarter, I decided to plan something special for the children: a Mother's Day tea. We put our heads together to come up with ideas of how to honor our mothers. We practiced singing and signing songs. We memorized a poem. We made sand candles and wrapped them in hand-stenciled, white paper bags tied with pretty ribbons. We wrote and decorated individual Mother's Day cards.

We decided to hold our tea the Friday before Mother's Day. Each child took home an invitation with an RSVP at the bottom. I was surprised and relieved to see that every mother was planning to attend. I even invited my own mother.

Finally, the big day arrived. At 1:45 that afternoon, each child lined up at our classroom door in anticipation of the arrival of his or her mom. As it got closer to starting time, I looked around and my eyes quickly found Jimmy. His mother hadn't shown up and he was looking stricken.

I took my mother by the hand and walked over to Jimmy. "Jimmy," I said, "I have a bit of a problem here and I was wondering if you could help out. I'm going to be really busy introducing our songs and our poem and pouring the punch. I was wondering if you could maybe keep my mother company while I'm busy. You could get her punch and cookies, and give her the candle I made when it's time."

My mom and Jimmy sat at a table with two other mother/child teams. Jimmy served my mom her treats, presented her with the gift I had made, and pulled out and pushed in her chair, just as we had practiced the day before. Whenever I looked over, my mother and Jimmy were in deep conversation.

I tucked that special memory away. Now, 10 years later, I work with students of all ages, educating them about the environment. Last year, I was at a high school to take a senior class on a field trip, and there was Jimmy.

We spent the day in the badlands of Montana. On the way back, I had the students complete an outline of the day's events, a short test and an evaluation of our trip. As I collected the student booklets, I checked them to see that everything was complete.

When I came to Jimmy's evaluation page, he had written, "Remember our Mother's Day tea we had in second grade, Mrs. Marra? I do! Thanks for all you did for me, and thank your mother, too."

As we began unloading at the school, Jimmy made sure he was the last one to go. I told him I really enjoyed what he had written. He looked rather embarrassed, mumbled his own thanks, and then turned to walk away. As my bus driver began pulling away from the curb, Jimmy ran back and knocked on the bus door. I thought he had forgotten something. He jumped back on board and gave me a big hug. "Thanks again, Mrs. Marra. No one even knew my mom didn't make it!"

I ended my work day with a hug from a teenage boy who had probably stopped hugging teachers years ago.

Nancy Noel Marra

6

CREATIVITY
AT WORK

*We all have the extraordinary coded within
us . . . waiting to be released.*

Jean Houston

The Adjustment

A smile is a curve that sets everything straight.

Phyllis Diller

Darrin was four years old. This was his first visit to the chiropractor. He was apprehensive, as most children are on their first visit to any doctor.

I learned early in my career that trying to adjust children without first gaining their confidence and trust resulted in screaming, running and bouncing off the walls. But if you gain children's confidence and take the time to develop a good relationship, you can do anything you want, with their complete cooperation. And it only need take a few moments.

One of the techniques I find most useful is to show an interest in a child's special toy. When you hold, touch, hug and love a favored toy, you open the door to the child's heart. I have given thousands of chiropractic adjustments to teddy bears, fire trucks, Barbie dolls, balloons, broken toys and Darth Vaders—you name it, I've adjusted it.

But Darrin's situation was different.

I had told Jean, Darrin's mother, to bring his favorite toy with him when she came to the office, but when I asked her what it was, she said, "Oh, Dr. Stillwagon, I couldn't bring it with me."

"Why?" I asked.

Jean replied, "You'll die when I tell you this, but Darrin's favorite play toy is our upright vacuum sweeper, and I just couldn't feel comfortable coming to the office with it."

"Wait just a minute," I said. I went down the hallway to the janitor's room and got our upright vacuum cleaner. I came running down the hall with it and into the adjusting room. The look in Darrin's eyes was enough to tell me that we were on the same wavelength, and we could very quickly become friends.

I introduced him to our vacuum cleaner, encouraging him to touch the bag and play with it while I adjusted his mother.

Our examination procedure involves the use of a hand-held, infrared scanning unit called the Derma Therm-O-Graph, which is used to monitor the patient's progress. After completing Jean's treatment, I took the instrument and ran the scanner the full length of the upright sweeper. I then placed the sweeper on the adjusting table and simulated a chiropractic adjustment on it.

Darrin watched my every move. I had him keep his hands on the sweeper while it was on the table. I told him that the sweeper would soon feel better.

Darrin was next. Full of confidence, he sat on the chair for the instrument scan, and fearlessly sat on the adjustment table. His confidence was complete. We had become friends, and I had adjusted my first upright vacuum cleaner!

G. Stillwagon, D.C., Ph.C.

"My chiropractor says I should find a branch that's more ergonomically correct."

Doing Good and Doing Well

*Excellent firms don't believe in excellence—
only in constant improvement and constant
change.*

Tom Peters

Quad/Graphics is one of the largest printing companies
in the world. It is the brainchild of Harry Quadracci Jr., a
natural genius in the field of employee self-enhancement.
He constantly searches for cheaper, faster and more wonderful ways to do business, always applying standards of
the highest integrity.

I was asked to do a four-day training for about 900 of
the company's managers. In preparation, I conducted a
set of pre-presentation telephone interviews with a ran-
domly selected group of employees. One of the most
interesting interviews was with John Imes, their ecology
manager. Since a huge printing plant can produce a lot of
waste, his job is to deal with all of Quad/Graphics' efflu-
ents. They were producing a considerable amount of
waste every day in every plant. John was brought in some

years ago to see what he could do to lower the costs associated with this waste, and to bring the plants into compliance with Environmental Protection Agency standards and regulations.

John told me he had come to the conclusion that, "We live in this town. If we spew anything into the air, we'll all breathe it and so will our children. If we pollute the streams, we'll all be drinking it." So he made up his mind that the company had to commit to cleaning it all up. However, in tune with Harry Quadracci's policies, he also decided that it had to be done while still making a profit.

Eight years later, they were actually making a profit from the cleanup efforts! They were also in full compliance with the EPA. The first thing John did was to call the EPA inspector and invite him into the plant. "I want you to be my partner in making this plant in full compliance. How can we work together to make that happen?" The inspector said that this kind of conversation had never happened before. John said to the inspector, "I want you here with me all the time. I don't want an adversarial relationship. I want to make this plant, and all our plants, clean, efficient and effective. Let's be partners in this process."

In looking at the various sources of potential pollution, the ink used in printing was a very large one. They discovered that inks could be made of soy. Up until that time, soy-based inks had various problems that made them impractical. John suggested to the company that they investigate this further. A few years later, they were in the soy ink business, had perfected soy-based inks, and were now supplying them all over the world.

Then, another breakthrough. They discovered that waste paper could be used in many profitable ways. Little by little, they discovered that there was a use—a profitable use—for almost everything that had been discarded previously. Where each plant had been producing many barrels of waste each day, they cut it down to less than one barrel per day.

For John Imes, every day has become an opportunity to do something of value—not only for his company, but for his community as well.

Hanoch McCarty, Ed.D.

Managing the Space Program

You cannot step into the same river twice.

Heraclitus

On October 4, 1957, the Soviets had launched Sputnik I, the first earth satellite, followed in less than a month by Sputnik II—this time with a live dog in the payload. With these launches the Soviet Union had leap-frogged into apparent technological supremacy in the race into space.

By 1958, the U.S.A. was supporting two parallel space efforts. One focused on the Redstone missile, developed by the Army's Ballistic Missile Agency; the other, centered on Thor, was an Air Force enterprise.

J. L. Jack Bromberg was head of the Thor program. The first three launches of the Thor Intermediate-Range Ballistic Missile failed, and in a mixture of desperation and hope, he hired Ted Gordon to write the countdown for the upcoming launches.

This was no simple task, as each launch of a Thor required that some 3,000 parts all function perfectly at the proper time. Among the last tests to be performed before launching was a switch set to operate the moment the missile lifted off, which locked open all the doors that allowed fuel to reach the engines. The switch was secured by a pin, to be removed by hand in the final seconds of countdown. But before the pin was to be removed, the switch was to be checked electrically to make sure it was not faulty.

One day, a multi-stage Thor was on the launch pad. Gordon, who was watching, saw to his horror the control panel light up, signaling that the first-stage main oxygen and fuel valves had suddenly opened. That meant kerosene and liquid oxygen were being fed into the rocket's combustion chamber, where they formed a combustible and highly explosive mixture. The mixture, having nowhere else to go, gushed out of the chamber and dropped to the launch pad many feet below. The mechanics and engineers working on the pad scattered in every direction. They were literally running for their lives, fleeing the holocaust that an accidental spark or electrical shock could ignite.

The spark never came. The potential inferno reduced itself to an oily mess.

Later, Gordon discovered that the mechanic in charge of testing the fuel switch had simply reversed the specified procedure. He had pulled the pin first.

The launch was rescheduled with no great difficulty, but had there been a spark, the explosion would have been catastrophic. The damage done to the public approval and congressional support of the budding space program might have resulted in no more Thor or Jupiter launches, no continued enthusiasm for NASA and no Neil Armstrong landing on the moon in 1969.

What to do about the mechanic?

Gordon recalls sitting around the launch pad with opinions flying thick and fast. "Fire him immediately."

"Suspend him with stiff penalties." "Transfer him." "Just get him out of there!"

Gordon listened and then delivered his opinion. "There's one thing we know about him for sure," he said. "He'll never, ever, as long as he lives, do anything like that again. Maybe he'll become our most reliable mechanic. Maybe we shouldn't fire him. Maybe we should promote him!"

In the end, that's what happened. The Thor test went forward as planned, the U.S. space program flourished, and it was not a Soviet but an American crew that reached the moon.

And never again did that mechanic blow a countdown.

Rushworth M. Kidder

"Maybe it was the red and black ones I wasn't supposed to cross."

Attention to Detail

A capacity for childlike wonder carried into adult life typifies the creative person.

Kaiser News

Just before opening the Pirates of the Caribbean ride at Disneyland, Walt Disney was touring the ride and felt strangely dissatisfied. In his heart he felt that something was missing, although he couldn't quite put his finger on what it was. He gathered as many employees as he could find—including the maintenance and food service personnel—and led them through a kind of sensual "tour de focus."

"Does it look right?" he asked. Yes, the costumes and shrubbery were authentic; the buildings had been copied from the New Orleans French Quarter, down to their intricate wrought-iron decorations. They all looked right.

"Does it sound right?" Disney had the latest in audio equipment installed to accurately reproduce the sounds of music, voices, boats and even animals that you'd associate with the Caribbean. Yes, it sounded right.

"Does it feel right?" He had controlled the temperature and humidity to exactly match that of a sultry New Orleans night. Yes, it felt right.

"Does it smell right?" An elaborate, smell-producing system had been created that could combine the smells of Cajun food with gunpowder, moss and brine. Yes, it smelled right.

And yet, something was still missing. "What is it?" Disney asked.

Finally, one of the young men who had been sweeping the floors said, "Well, Mr. Disney, I grew up in the South, and what strikes me is that on a summer night like this, there ought to be lightning bugs." Disney's face lit up. That, of course, was it! The young man was given a generous bonus, and Disney actually had live lightning bugs shipped in until he could figure out a way to imitate them mechanically.

Bryan W. Mattimore

"Move Over!"

When we love and laugh with our patient, we elevate the highest degree of healing, which is inner peace.

Leslie Gibson

The nursing staff at a nearby hospital was having trouble with an aged man's difficult temperament. He refused to allow anyone into his room and was often so negative that staff members could not even administer medication. One day, an insightful nurse decided to ask a friend of hers to make a difference in this man's life.

That evening, while the man lay quietly glowering in his bed, the door slowly opened into his dimly lit room. As his eyes shot toward the doorway, ready to command a dismissal, he was struck by a figure that stood silently staring at him. It was not the usual "intrusive" staff member, but instead, a circus clown. His features shimmering with face paint, the character sprinted to the patient's bedside. "Move over!" he shouted.

Startled by the order, the old man slid aside as the

clown climbed into bed with him. Adjusting the blankets, the clown settled in. He began paging through a book he had brought. "I'm going to read to you," he said. Then he began: "Jack and Jill went up the hill to fetch a pail of water. Jack fell down and broke his crown and Jill came tumbling after." The clown continued on through the collection of Mother Goose as the man listened intently, his body calming with each page. By the end of the reading, the once sullen old man lay nestled against his playful visitor, feeling a sense of peace no staff member had ever witnessed. The clown kissed the man on his forehead and said good-bye.

That night, the patient quietly and effortlessly moved into the next life, his face showing contentment and peace.

Jeffrey Patnaude

"I understand your computer is down. I'm here to cheer it up."

Reprinted with permission from Harley Schwadron.

Search for a Smile and Share It

If you're not using your smile, you're like a man with a million dollars in the bank and no checkbook.

Les Giblin

It was a typical Wednesday. My wife and I were speaking in a nursing home about our successful recovery from a heart attack. Afterward, one of the residents, Miriam, asked if we had a few minutes to talk.

"I've always thought to be happy I need three things: someone to love, something to do and something to look forward to," she said. "I've got people here to love, and the activities keep me as busy as I want, but I don't have anything I'm looking forward to. Do you have any ideas?"

"What did you look forward to before you came here?" we asked.

"Oh, I used to love to laugh with others," Miriam said.

"What did you laugh about?" we asked.

"Everything I could see, hear, feel, taste or smell," she said with a smile.

At that very moment, we got the idea to start our project. We began looking for humor, and we used all of our senses.

We started with a poster that said: *Life is too important to be taken seriously.* We found a button that read: *Enjoy life. This is not a dress rehearsal.* On a teabag was the message: *You are like this tea bag . . . only in hot water do you realize how strong you are.*

We continued searching and found cartoons, videos and audiocassettes filled with humor. People brought us bumper stickers, illustrations, books, games, comic strips and magazines. We put together humor baskets with books, tapes, greeting cards and toys for children of all ages. Stuffed animals were ever popular, followed by Slinkies and Kusch balls. And no basket was complete without bubbles to blow.

Of course, we made a humor basket for Miriam, the woman who had started us on this project. She told us that the highlight of her day was sharing the contents of her basket with others: residents, visitors . . . anyone she saw. Someone said what she was doing was searching for a smile and sharing it. So, that's what we called our project, "Search for a Smile and Share it."

The project was so successful that other facilities got wind of it and made special requests.

One nursing home asked us to make a humor cart, like a shopping cart. Volunteers push this down the hallways, sharing smiles and laughs with many residents. Still another nursing home requested that we design a humor room, complete with a VCR for fun videos. Soon families began donating favorite videos like Sports Bloopers, Candid Camera, and Carol Burnett and Johnny Carson skits.

What started as a simple gesture to help one elderly woman turned into a lifetime project.

Miriam has gone to her final reward now, but when we last saw her she had a sign on her nursing home door: *Happy Is the Woman Who Can Laugh at Herself. She Shall Never Cease to Be Amused.*

John Murphy

The name Miriam is a pseudonym.

Getting the Garbage Out

The invariable mark of wisdom is to see the miraculous in the common.

Ralph Waldo Emerson

When architect Jaime Lerner was appointed mayor of Curitiba, Brazil, in 1973, it was a rapidly growing town of 500,000 with sprawling *favelas* (slums). The *favelas* had many problems, not the least of which was garbage that could not be collected because of narrow or non-existing streets.

Since trucks could not get in, and because the garbage was attracting rodents that could carry disease, Lerner had to come up with a way to get the garbage out. His solution was to pay people for their garbage by placing recycling bins around the *favelas* and giving the people tokens to the city's transport system for the separated and, therefore, recyclable trash. For organic waste, which was taken by farmers and made into fertilizer for their fields, he gave chits that could be exchanged for food.

It has worked spectacularly. Kids scour the *favelas* for trash, and can spot the difference between polyethylene terephthalate and high-density polyethylene bottles. The tokens give the poorer citizens the means to get out of the *favelas* to where the jobs are, while promoting cleanliness, frugality, and the reclaiming and recycling of waste.

Paul Hawken

Time Out

The present time has one advantage over every other—it is our own.

Charles C. Colton

He was the president of a major advertising firm and I was a very young management consultant. I had been recommended to him by one of his employees who had seen my work and thought I had something to offer. I was nervous. At that stage in my career, it wasn't very often that I got to talk to the president of a company.

The appointment was at 10:00 A.M., for one hour. I arrived early. Promptly at 10, I was ushered into a large and airy room, with furniture upholstered in bright yellow.

He had his shirtsleeves rolled up and a mean look on his face.

"You've only got 20 minutes," he barked.

I sat there, not saying a word.

"I said, you've only got 20 minutes."

Again, not a word.

"Your time's ticking away. Why aren't you saying anything?"

"They're my 20 minutes," I replied. "I can do whatever I want with them."

He burst into laughter.

We then spoke for an hour and a half. I got the job.

Martin Rutte

Poetic Vision

We are ourselves, creations. And we, in turn, are meant to continue creativity by being creative.

Julia Cameron

Our organization, the Meteorological Association of New Zealand Limited, had just gone through a period of intense change, moving from being a government department to an independent, thriving and expanding weather forecasting business. We had no models to follow, and it was very clear to us that what our whole organization needed was the power of a shared vision.

In the government days, the approach had been to reduce costs by computerizing everything in sight. This was particularly true in the forecast room. Although the work practices in the forecast room didn't undergo much change when we left the government, we decided to change the philosophy behind the work. We stressed that people, not computers, were in charge of the forecast process, supported by good systems and equipment. We had not yet put this philosophy to work, and the time had come to have a vision statement for the forecast process.

So, after strenuous debate and thrashing out of the basic issues, a set of fine words emerged—workmanlike, but hardly riveting.

> *A forecast service exploiting information with skill
> and effective techniques, in an inspiring environment,
> for the benefit of the customers.*

As we sat around the table, administrators, professors and forecasters, struggling to find a way to communicate this vision to the rest of the company, a man named Marco cleared his throat and read:

> *We exploit information on weather*
> *With techniques that grow ever better*
> *Our inspiring environment*
> *And high skill requirement*
> *Make our customers love us forever.*

Silence. Someone took Marco's paper and copied the verse on the board. The laughter broke out, as well as enthusiastic cries of, "That's it!"

We still smile when we refer to it. Even the board of directors smiled. And changes are happening consistent with its meaning. In one moment, we moved from boring and proper to fun and effective!

John Lumsden

"Management thinks I can offer a new perspective."

7

OVERCOMING OBSTACLES

It is our duty as men and women to proceed as though the limits of our abilities do not exist.

Pierre Teilhard de Chardin

Reprinted with permission from Harley Schwadron.

How to Get Their Attention

Nothing ever succeeds which exuberant spirits have not helped to produce.

Nietzsche

Several years ago, I was dean of the Lansing School of Nursing, Education and Health Sciences at Bellarmine College in Louisville, Kentucky. The school was located on the top of a hill. All the other administrative and academic buildings were on another hill.

One day in late January, we had a severe ice storm followed by snow. The grounds maintenance crew did a masterful job cleaning the main part of the campus, but they "forgot" our hill and the Lansing School. When I arrived at the office, I found myself confronted with 200 irate students, 12 hysterical faculty and 4 staff members. Neither the hill nor the parking lot had been cleared.

I had two immediate challenges facing me: get the hill cleaned and lower the stress level of all involved. I had faced this situation two months before; when I had called the physical plant office, I had been told they'd get to us when they could.

This time I asked my secretary for a purchase order form and check request form. I then typed up a purchase order for a ski lift from Switzerland. Since I had no idea how much a small ski lift cost, I put down $600,000. I figured I could get something for that amount. Then I requested $60,000 as the required deposit. To this day, I have no idea of the procedure for such a purchase, but it didn't matter—I was making it all up.

I photocopied the forms and posted copies throughout the school. Then I hand-delivered the bogus requests directly to the executive vice-president's office, since he was the authority over physical plant operations. I informed his secretary that this was very important and I needed an answer ASAP.

Within minutes of returning to my office, I received an irate phone call.

"Have you lost your mind?" thundered the executive vice-president. "We can't afford this! Who authorized you to order a ski lift?"

"The president," I answered meekly.

I'm told he slammed down his phone, went charging down the hall, requisition in hand, burst into the president's office and demanded, "Did you authorize this?"

The president, who knew me well, took his time reading the purchase order. Then he slowly looked up and said, "You didn't clean her hill, did you?"

"Why didn't she just say so?" the vice president spluttered.

The president laughed. "She certainly got your attention, didn't she?"

Within 10 minutes we had snowplows and salt trucks up on our hill. Everyone was at the windows, laughing and cheering.

Dr. Ann E. Weeks

Attitude Is Everything

Jerry was the kind of guy you love to hate. He was always in a good mood and always had something positive to say. When someone would ask him how he was doing, he would reply, "If I were any better, I would be twins!"

He was a unique manager because he had several waiters who had followed him around from restaurant to restaurant. The reason the waiters followed Jerry was because of his attitude. He was a natural motivator. If an employee was having a bad day, Jerry was there telling the employee how to look on the positive side of the situation.

Seeing this style really made me curious, so one day I went up to Jerry and asked him, "I don't get it! You can't be a positive, up person all the time. How do you do it?"

Jerry replied, "Each morning I wake up and say to myself, 'Jerry you have two choices today. You can choose to be in a good mood or you can choose to be in a bad mood.' I choose to be in a good mood. Each time something bad happens, I can choose to be a victim or I can choose to learn from it. I choose to learn from it. Every time someone comes to me complaining, I can choose to accept their complaining or I can point out the positive side of life. I choose the positive side of life."

"Yeah, right, it's not that easy," I protested.

"Yes it is," Jerry said. "Life is all about choices. When you cut away all the junk, every situation is a choice. You choose how you react to situations. You choose how people will affect your mood. You choose to be in a good or bad mood. The bottom line: it's your choice how you live life."

I reflected on what Jerry said. Soon thereafter, I left the restaurant industry to start my own business. We lost touch, but I often thought about him when I made a choice about life instead of reacting to it.

Several years later, I heard that Jerry did something you are never supposed to do in the restaurant business: he left the back door open one morning and was held up at gunpoint by three armed robbers. While trying to open the safe, his hand, shaking from nervousness, slipped off the combination. The robbers panicked and shot him. Luckily, Jerry was found relatively quickly and rushed to the local trauma center. After 18 hours of surgery and weeks of intensive care, Jerry was released from the hospital with fragments of the bullets still in his body.

I saw Jerry about six months after the accident. When I asked him how he was, he replied, "If I were any better, I'd be twins. Wanna see my scars?" I declined to see his wounds, but did ask him what had gone through his mind as the robbery took place.

"The first thing that went through my mind was that I should have locked the back door," Jerry replied. "Then, as I lay on the floor, I remembered that I had two choices: I could choose to live, or I could choose to die. I chose to live."

"Weren't you scared? Did you lose consciousness?" I asked.

Jerry continued, "The paramedics were great. They kept telling me I was going to be fine. But when they wheeled me into the emergency room and I saw the expressions on the faces of the doctors and nurses, I got really scared. In their eyes, I read, 'He's a dead man.' I knew I needed to take action."

"What did you do?" I asked.

"Well, there was a big, burly nurse shouting questions at me," said Jerry. "She asked if I was allergic to anything. 'Yes,' I replied. The doctors and nurses stopped working as they waited for my reply. I took a deep breath and yelled, 'Bullets!' Over their laughter, I told them, 'I am choosing to live. Operate on me as if I am alive, not dead.'"

Jerry lived thanks to the skill of his doctors, but also because of his amazing attitude. I learned from him that every day we have the choice to live fully. Attitude, after all, is everything.

Francie Baltazar-Schwartz

Leading the Charge!

Many years ago there was a huge oil refinery fire. Flames shot hundreds of feet into the air. The sky was thick with grimy black smoke. The heat was intense—so intense that firefighters had to park their trucks a block away and wait for the heat to die down before they could begin to fight the fire. However, it was about to rage out of control.

Then, all of a sudden, from several blocks away came a fire truck racing down the street. With its brakes screeching, it hit the curb in front of the fire. The firefighters jumped out and began to battle the blaze. All the firefighters who were parked a block away saw this, and they jumped into their trucks, drove down the block and began to fight the fire, too. As a result of that cooperative effort, they were just barely able to bring the fire under control.

The people who saw this teamwork thought, "My goodness, the man who drove that lead fire truck—what an act of bravery!" They decided to give him a special award to recognize him for his bravery in leading the charge.

At the ceremony the mayor said, "Captain, we want to honor you for a fantastic act of bravery. You prevented the loss of property, perhaps even the loss of life. If there is one special thing you could have—just about anything—what would it be?"

Without hesitation, the captain replied, "Your Honor, a new set of brakes would be dandy!"

Mike Wickett

The Phantom

What we need is more people who specialize in the impossible.

Theodore Roethke

In the winter of 1963, my 23rd year of life, I found myself in the U.S. Navy as the Combat Information Center officer aboard a destroyer, USS *Eaton*.

A day out of Cape Hatteras, the outer fringes of a hurricane coming up the coast began to nibble at us. Then it pounced. For three days it mauled us, nearly sweeping me overboard at one point. For three days I vomited. Then on November 29, the hurricane released us. We licked our wounds for a day and made repairs.

The following day, a Phantom jet crashed into the water.

I had intended to offer the Navy my services as the pilot of just such an airplane. But when my left eye went 20/40 during my senior year at Roanoke, my dreams of being a naval aviator ended. Someone suggested I could still fly by becoming a radar intercept officer, or RIO, the person who rides behind the pilot and operates the attack radar. It seemed like a great idea until I learned that the RIO also handles all the radio communication.

You see, the big problem—*the secret*—was that I was a stutterer. The toughest words were those beginning with hard sounds, like t or b, k or g. I lived with a chronic, low-grade fear of stuttering. I decided to avoid the potential ignominy of being required to handle radio communication from a jet and take my chances on a destroyer, where, I hoped, I wouldn't have to talk so much.

Of course, the Navy, in its infinite wisdom, made me an air controller. That is how, just weeks out of training, green at the gills after a hurricane, I came to be standing watch in the middle of the night when a voice as deep as God's came over the radio.

"Hermit," said the voice, "this is Climax Himself. Over."

"Hermit" was my ship's call sign. "Climax" was the call sign of the most formidable ship in the fleet, the aircraft carrier USS *Enterprise*, flagship of the battle group we were escorting across the Atlantic. "Climax Himself" was the *Enterprise's* captain. My heart pounded.

"Hermit, we just lost a Foxtrot Four out your way," he said. "Both men are down and missing." Translation: The Phantom jet had crashed, and our ship was being deputized on the spot as search-and-rescue coordinator because we were the ship nearest the plane's last known position. That meant that it was my sudden duty to be responsible for coordinating the search.

It would have been hard to find a more difficult word for me to pronounce than "Climax." And, fresh out of Air Control School, I had never been responsible for a real live airplane in my life. Nevertheless, with a determination born of grim images of two souls out there in the frigid water, I took a grease pencil, donned headphones and sat down at my radar console.

When we graduated from Air Control School, they told

us we most likely would never have to control more than four or five aircraft at a time. I now had a conversation going with 15 to 20 planes, all streaming toward a potentially disastrous convergence at the center of my scope. Out of the inky night the voices started coming in to me in the laid-back, relaxed, under-pressure argot of Navy pilots: "Ah, Roger, Hermit, this is Climax two-three. I have two-four and two-five in tow. Request vector. Over." The dialogue went on like that for almost 24 hours.

Three or four hours into the ordeal, it flashed on me that I was not stuttering. Not only was I not stuttering, I hadn't even thought about it. I'll never forget the feelings of amazement, exhilaration, grace and gratitude that swept over me at that moment. It occurred to me that in that situation it simply was "not authorized" for me to stutter—not with those two guys down out there and depending on me. I was almost overwhelmed several times with the awareness that this was surely a spiritual experience, a life-changing swerve in the road, a release from captivity, a moment of birth.

As the only controller on our little ship qualified to control jets, I had to stay on the scope as night turned into day and then into the night once more.

At about sunup the following day, one of the search planes got a fix on a rescue beacon . . . but found only fragments of the RIO's helmet and ejection seat. But then a little later, another plane spotted the pilot bobbing in the swells. We steamed toward the plane, but Climax Himself sent a helicopter from *Enterprise* to bring his pilot home and called over to me to say, "Bravo Zulu, Hermit." That's Navy talk for "well done!"

We arrived at the scene shortly after the helicopter and its rescue crew. As the pilot was being helped into the sling, he somehow got a message to our ship. Our captain's voice came over the speaker: "Mister Scherer, lay to the bridge! Some guy out there wants to see you." The sun was just coming up as I ran up the short ladder. The helicopter hovered 20 feet above the water, the pilot just beginning to rise.

We looked at each other over the water. I grinned, waved and gave him a thumbs-up. Dangling from the hoist, just before he disappeared into the helicopter, the water-logged pilot took a last, long hard look—then saluted me. Standing there on *Eaton's* rolling deck, I returned his salute. And I wept. I had helped find his Phantom. He had no way of knowing that he had also helped me find mine.

John Scherer

Staying Motivated

A new idea is first condemned as ridiculous, and then dismissed as trivial, until finally it becomes what everybody knows.

William James

"That would never work in our business!" Jeff exclaimed. "We sell medical equipment to doctors and it is a tough market. Our salespeople don't have but 10 or 15 minutes on a call, and they have to be hard and move fast."

Jeff, a participant in one of my sales management seminars, was responding to my suggestion that managers should explore ways to help their salespeople stay motivated. I had mentioned some activities in connection with pre-call preparation, such as reading a chapter from a motivational book, listening to a motivation tape in the car, or using affirmations. "I'm telling you, that touchy-feely stuff won't work in our business," Jeff repeated.

But 10 days later I received a telephone call from Jeff, inviting me to speak at his company's annual sales meeting. Again, he cautioned me about how tough his market was and how hardened and caustic his salespeople were.

My presentation went well, and I found Jeff's sales force similar in most respects to the typical sales force I work with. Jeff was right in one regard—they were a little uptight and defensive.

As I began to discuss ideas they could use to get more focused and motivated, Jeff rolled his eyes. I could read his thoughts: "Oh, no. This will never work!" The group stirred uneasily as I challenged them to think about the possibilities of positive programming.

I asked if any of them had any "little tricks" they used to prepare themselves for their calls. From the back of the room, Bruce raised his hand. "I do." The room fell absolutely dead silent. Bruce was the newest salesperson on the team—he had been there only a few months—and was killing everyone else. He was the company's top salesperson.

"I get very nervous before I make a call," Bruce said. "I don't want to screw up. So there is this little routine I go through before every call."

"Would you tell us about it?" I asked.

"Sure," he said. "I sit in my car for a few minutes and do this breathing exercise. Would it be all right if I showed you?"

Bruce pulled his chair out so everyone could see, sat down, and described how he breathed in good, blue air right up through the soles of his feet, up through his legs and into his lungs. Then he exhaled red air, taking all the tension and nervousness out of his body. He replaced all the tension with positive affirmations until all the air going out was blue, too. He breathed in and exhaled with a very audible, "Ummmm . . ." He repeated this process several times, then said, "Well, that's what I do."

No one in the room said anything. I glanced at Jeff, who looked as though he was about to pass out. "Don't you dare say anything about what I said," his body language told me. I would have loved to say, "Yanh, yanh, yanh. See. I told you so!" In fact, I never mentioned it to him. I think he got the message.

I thanked Bruce and asked if any of the others had something they did to prepare for their calls. David, the company's second leading salesperson and the one who had the Manhattan territory in New York—the "toughest territory in the company"—stood up. He described how he played a particular Mozart piece on his car CD player to help him relax, focus and "build confidence and determination inside myself." Then two other participants shared what they did to prepare for a sales call.

About a year later, I received a great letter from the president of Jeff's company, describing their sales increases since the meeting and thanking me for my contribution. He referred to some of the sales techniques we presented. But I am convinced the most important lessons from that meeting, and the ones that made the most difference, came from the participants themselves.

Mike Stewart

Reprinted with permission by Randy Glasbergen.

We Will Survive

Never, never, never, never give up.

Winston Churchill

When I took over the job as general director of the New York City Opera in 1979, every bit of financial information was uniformly bad. Dozens of creditors were calling. We owed everybody—even Lincoln Center, where we performed.

In my first year as general director I raised $5 million, which was $1.5 million less than what we lost. I was focusing so hard on the money plight that I almost forgot why I'd wanted the job to begin with—to produce operas.

The first one I got involved with was *Silverlake,* presented in March 1980. Broadway producer Hal Prince was brought in to direct, and Joel Grey was cast in the lead.

On opening night Hal gave me a plant that I placed on a little wooden stand in my office. Within a week the plant died. That really bothered me. One of its leaves was still green, so I clipped it off, chucked the plant in a wastebasket and then planted the leaf. I took very good care of that leaf. I watered it every day and left it under a lamp at night. I made sure everyone knew that lamp had to stay on at night. I then pasted the headline of a newspaper article about me across the bottom of the pot. The headline read: "I WON'T BE DEFEATED"—BEVERLY SILLS' INDOMITABLE SPIRIT IS INFUSING NEW LIFE INTO THE NEW YORK CITY OPERA.

Everyone who worked in our underground warren thought I had lost my mind over that leaf. But pretty soon they all started coming by to water it. I know this will strike you as a little crazy, but everybody really started rooting for that little leaf to live. I don't know how long we kept it up, but one morning when I walked in, another little shoot had come up through the soil. A couple of days later another one appeared, and then another after that, and eventually that leaf became a lovely, healthy plant that's alive and well in my basement office of the New York City Opera. You don't have to tell me how dumb it was for a group of intelligent people to identify with a leaf, but we did. That leaf survived. The New York City Opera would survive. It *had* to.

Beverly Sills
From Beverly, *by Beverly*
Sills and Lawrence Linderman

Credit, Not Charity

Great things are done by people who think great thoughts and then go out into the world to make their dreams come true.

Ernest Holmes

The Grameen Bank began out of the pocket of one man, Dr. Mohammad Yunus. His story begins in 1972, the year after Bangladesh won its war of liberation from Pakistan. Dr. Yunus had recently completed his graduate studies at Vanderbilt University in the United States and was teaching at a college in Tennessee, when he was invited to take up the position of head of the economics department at Chittagong University in southeastern Bangladesh.

He arrived home full of the high hopes that followed independence. But to his surprise, the country was sliding downward very rapidly. By 1974, there was a terrible famine and people were dying in the streets. Dr. Yunus was teaching development economics and was becoming increasingly frustrated with the difference between what was described in the classroom and what was occurring in the real world. So he decided to learn economics the way the real world is, the economics that were real in people's lives.

Because Chittagong University is located among villages, Dr. Yunus was able to walk out of the campus into real Bangladesh. He began going to the villages and talking to the poor people, trying to discover why they couldn't change their lives or their living conditions. He did not approach them as a teacher or a researcher, but as a human being, a neighbor.

One day he came across a woman who earned only two pennies a day by making bamboo stools. He couldn't believe how anyone could work so hard and make only two pennies a day. When he questioned her, he discovered that she didn't have enough money to buy the bamboo from the bamboo store, so she had to borrow money from a trader—the same trader who bought the final product. When the trader bought her stools, he offered her a price that barely covered her materials. In essence, her labor was almost free; she worked like a slave.

"Well," he thought, "this isn't difficult to solve." If the money was available for her to buy her own bamboo, she could sell the product wherever she could get a good price. Dr. Yunus and a student went around the village for several days to find out if there were other people like her who were borrowing from traders and missing out on what they should earn. In a week's time they came up with a list of 42 such people. The total amount needed by all 42 of them was $30.

His first solution was to take the $30 out of his pocket. He asked the student to distribute the money to them as loans. But then he saw that this was not a real solution because when other villagers needed money, they wouldn't come to him, since he was a teacher at the university. He was not in the money business. That's when he thought of a bank.

He approached a bank manager, who thought it too funny an idea even to talk about. Loans of that amount weren't even worth the paperwork, he said, plus the poor people didn't have any collateral. Dr. Yunus went from bank to bank, receiving the same response. Finally he challenged the bank by offering himself as guarantor. After six months, they reluctantly agreed to a $300 loan.

He loaned the money and it was paid back. Again, he asked the bank to loan the money directly, and again they declined, saying it would never work in more than one village. Dr. Yunus persevered. He loaned money over several villages. It worked, but the bankers still weren't satisfied. So he finally loaned money over a whole district. And still it worked, and still the bankers were not persuaded.

Finally Dr. Yunus said, "Why am I running after these bankers? Why don't I set up my own bank and just settle this issue?" So in 1983, the government gave permission to set up a bank, and this bank is now called Grameen Bank. It lends money only to the poorest people in Bangladesh—landless, assetless people.

Today, Grameen Bank has 1,048 branches and over 2 million borrowers. They work in 35,000 villages. The bank has disbursed over a billion dollars, the average loan being about $150. The bank not only lends money to the poor people; it is owned by the poor people. The people that are lent money become shareholders in the bank. Out of the 2 million borrowers, 90 percent are women, something previously unheard of in Bangladesh.

The bank has been emulated around the world. Dr. Yunus stresses that at every point of the way, he was told that it could not be done and that there were very compelling reasons why it could not be done. But the reality of the situation is that it *is* being done, and in brilliant and unexpected ways.

*Excerpted from a speech by and radio
interview with Mohammad Yunus in* Lapis Magazine

The Question

Press on! A better fate awaits you.

Victor Hugo

Isn't it amazing how few of us ask ourselves the important question?

Several years ago I was invited to hear an important speaker address the student body of a small college in South Carolina. The auditorium was filled with students excited about the opportunity to hear a person of her stature speak. After the governor gave the introduction, the speaker moved to the microphone, looked at the audience from left to right, and began:

"I was born to a mother who was deaf and could not speak. I do not know who my father is or was. The first job I ever had was in a cotton field."

The audience was spellbound. "Nothing has to remain the way it is if that's not the way a person wants it to be," she continued. "It isn't luck, and it isn't circumstances, and it isn't being born a certain way that causes a person's future to become what it becomes." And she softly repeated, "Nothing has to remain the way it is if that's not the way a person wants it to be.

"All a person has to do," she added in a firm voice, "to change a situation that brings unhappiness or dissatisfaction is answer the question: 'How do I want this situation to become?' Then the person must commit totally to personal actions that carry them there."

Then a beautiful smile shone forth as she said, "My name is Azie Taylor Morton. I stand before you today as treasurer of the United States of America."

Bob Moore

Tony Trivisonno's American Dream

Effort only releases its reward after a person refuses to quit.

Napoleon Hill

He came from a rocky farm in Italy, somewhere south of Rome. How or when he got to America, I don't know. But one evening I found him standing in the driveway behind my garage. He was about five-foot-seven or -eight, and thin.

"I mow your lawn," he said. It was hard to comprehend his broken English.

I asked him his name. "Tony Trivisonno," he replied. "I mow your lawn." I told Tony that I couldn't afford a gardener.

"I mow your lawn," he said again, then walked away. I went into my house unhappy. Yes, these Depression days were difficult, but how could I turn away a person who had come to me for help?

When I got home from work the next evening, the lawn had been mowed, the garden weeded and the walks raked. I asked my wife what had happened.

"A man got the lawn mower out of the garage and worked on the yard," she answered. "I assumed you had hired him." I told her of my experience the night before. We thought it strange that he had not asked for pay.

The next two days were busy, and I forgot about Tony. We were trying to rebuild our business and bring some of our workers back to the plants. But on Friday, returning home early, I saw Tony again, behind the garage. I complimented him on the work he had done.

"I mow your lawn," he said. I managed to work out some kind of small weekly pay, and each day Tony cleaned up the yard and took care of the little chores. My wife said he was very helpful whenever there were any heavy objects to lift or things to fix.

Summer passed into fall, and the winds blew cold. "Mr. Craw, snow pretty soon," Tony told me one evening. "When winter come, you give me job shoveling snow at the factory."

Well, what do you do with such persistence and hope? Of course, Tony got his job at the factory.

The months passed. I asked the personnel department for a report. They said Tony was a very good worker.

One day I found Tony at our meeting place behind the garage. "I want to be 'prentice," he said.

We had a pretty good apprentice school that trained laborers. But I doubted whether Tony had the capacity to read blueprints and micrometers or to do precision work. Still, how could I turn him down?

Tony took a cut in pay to become an apprentice. Months later, I got a report that he had graduated as a skilled grinder. He had learned to read the millionths of an inch on the micrometer and to true the grinding wheel with an instrument set with a diamond. My wife and I were delighted with what we felt was a satisfying end to the story.

A year or two passed, and again I found Tony in his usual waiting place. We talked about his work, and I asked him what he wanted.

"Mr. Craw," he said, "I like buy a house." On the edge of town, he had found a house for sale, a complete wreck.

I called on a banker friend. "Do you ever loan money on character?" I asked.

"No," he said. "We can't afford to. No sale."

"Now, wait a minute," I replied. "Here is a hard-working man, a man of character. I can vouch for that. He's got a good job. You're not getting a damn thing from your lot. He will stay there for years. At least he will pay you interest."

Reluctantly, the banker wrote a mortgage for $2,000 and gave Tony the house with no down payment. Tony was thrilled. From then on, any discarded odds and ends around our place—a broken screen, a bit of hardware, boards from packing—Tony would gather and take home.

After about two years, I found Tony in our familiar meeting spot. He seemed to stand a little straighter. He was heavier. He had a look of confidence.

"Mr. Craw, I sell my house!" he said with pride. "I got $8,000."

I was amazed. "But Tony, how are you going to live without a house?"

"Mr. Craw, I buy a farm."

We sat down and talked. Tony told me that to own a farm was his dream. He loved the tomatoes and peppers and all the other vegetables important to his Italian diet. He had sent for his wife and son and daughter back in Italy. He had hunted around the edge of town until he found a small, abandoned piece of property with a house and shed. Now he was moving his family to his farm.

Sometime later, Tony arrived on a Sunday afternoon, neatly dressed. He had another Italian man with him. He told me that he had persuaded his childhood friend to move to America. Tony was sponsoring him. With a twinkle in his eye, he told me that when they approached the little farm he now operated, his friend stood in amazement and said, "Tony, you are a millionaire!"

Then during the war, a message came from my company. Tony had passed away.

I asked our people to check on his family and see that everything was properly handled. They found the farm green with vegetables, the little house livable and homey. There was a tractor and a good car in the yard. The children were educated and working, and Tony didn't owe one red cent.

After he passed away, I thought more and more about Tony's career. He grew in stature in my mind. In the end, I think he stood as tall and as proud as the greatest American industrialist.

They had all reached their success by the same route, and by the same values and principles: vision, perseverance, determination, self-control, optimism, self-respect and, above all, integrity.

Tony did not begin on the bottom rung of the ladder. He began in the basement. Tony's affairs were tiny; the great industrialists' affairs were giant, but the balance sheets were exactly the same. The only difference was where you put your decimal point.

Tony Trivisonno came to America seeking the American dream. But he didn't find it—he created it for himself. All he had were 24 precious hours a day, and he wasted none of them.

Frederick C. Crawford

The Great Dill Deal

Comedy is acting out optimism.

Robin Williams

My parents, God bless them, lived through the Holocaust as children. After coming to America in 1947, my father labored in a sweat shop so that they could start a fruit and vegetable stand.

Their childhood experience did not include cooking lessons, so my parents only learned to cook as adults in America. My father's single culinary accomplishment was making hard-boiled eggs, and even those he usually mistimed. My mother easily outdistanced my father. She could, when pressed, cook seven different meals—but in reality, there were only two she made well: spaghetti and meatballs, thanks to the patient Italian grandmothers in our neighborhood, and a great pot of chicken soup. As she had access to all the vegetables in what was now our store, she would toss unusual ones, such as parsnips and parsley root, into the mix. But what distinguished Mom's chicken soup from any other I've tasted was one special ingredient: fresh dill.

Mom always made her chicken soup at the right time. Rarely did she make it for someone already sick; yet she knew instinctively when you needed some as preventive medicine. Somehow she also knew when hard times were coming. When a slew of salesmen would arrive, all demanding payment, there was a soul-soothing pot of chicken soup. Let the refrigerator break down, the tax man call, the employees leave without notice! We had chicken soup with fresh dill and we would be okay!

Many years later, my parents' store on Long Island burnt to the ground. They had no choice but to give up the retail trade and concentrate on building their fledgling wholesale produce business in New York City. They did so with their customary passion, and in a few years were doing pretty well. They specialized in carrying unusual and gourmet items—including fresh dill.

One winter, primarily for their health, they took a vacation. My brother and I flew to New York to help run the business while they were gone. It just so happened that in the second week, a freeze struck the South and virtually the entire fresh dill crop was wiped out. Demand for dill was enormous. You could practically hear the screams of distraught mothers from a hundred miles away.

Serendipitously, my brother and I had connections. We had lived in California and we knew the few dill growers there. In a matter of hours, we had arranged a stream of air shipments of dill to New York. We had the only dill in town, and although the supplies were still small, we made thousands upon thousands in profits—from dill!

When my parents returned from vacation, tanned and delighted to have missed some of the nastiest weather New York had seen in decades, they were especially happy to hear the story of the Great Dill Deal.

A few winters later, my brother and I had a business that was getting into real trouble. We became very worried, forgetting that business has its vicissitudes (the one big fancy word my dad knew and consequently used often), and that business isn't the only thing in life.

One afternoon when we were feeling especially downtrodden, a package from our folks arrived, sent from their new home in the Dominican Republic.

There was no letter, only a beautiful, custom-made wood plaque with a hand-carved message: NO BIG DILL. And you know what? After that, it really wasn't.

The Reverend Aaron Zerah

A Journey of Friendship

In the presence of love, miracles happen.

Robert Schuller

Curt and I have the kind of friendship that I wish everyone would be able to experience. It embodies the true meaning of partnership—trust, caring, risk-taking and all else that friendship could embrace in our hurried and harried lives.

Our friendship began many years ago. We met while attending different high schools, through competitive sports, and we had a mutual respect for each other's athletic abilities. As the years progressed, we became the best of friends. Curt was best man in my wedding, and I was his a few years later when he married my sister's roommate. He is also the godfather of my son, Nicholas. And yet the event that most exemplifies our partnership and solidified our friendship happened over 25 years ago, when we were young and in our carefree 20s.

Curt and I were attending a pool party at the local Swim and Racquet Club. He had just won the door prize, a beautiful new watch. We were walking to the car, joking about the party, and Curt turned to me and said, "Steve, you've had a few cocktails, buddy—maybe I should drive." At first I thought he was joking, but since Curt is definitely the wiser of us, I respected his sober judgment.

"Good idea," I said, and handed him the keys.

Once I was settled in the passenger seat and Curt behind the wheel, he said, "I'm going to need your help because I'm not sure how to get to your house from here."

"No problem," I responded.

Curt started the car and we were off—not without the usual first-time shifting jerks and stalls, stops and starts. The next 10 miles seemed like a hundred as I prompted Curt with directions—left now, slow down, right pretty soon, speed up and so on. The important thing is that we got home safely that night.

Ten years later at my wedding, Curt brought tears to the eyes of 400 guests as he told the story of our partnership and how we drove home together that night. Why such a remarkable story? We've all, I hope, offered our keys when we knew we shouldn't drive. But you see, my friend Curt is blind. He has been since birth and never sat behind the wheel of a car before that night.

Today, Curt is one of the top executives at General Motors in New York, and I travel around the country inspiring salespeople to form long-lasting partnerships and friendships with their clients. Our willingness to take risks and trust in each other continues to bring meaning and joy to the journey of friendship.

Steven B. Wiley

8

ON COURAGE

Don't be afraid to go out on a limb.
That's where the fruit is.

Anonymous

Billy

All of the significant battles are waged within the self.

Sheldon Koggs

A number of years ago (1983-1987), I had the opportunity to play the character of Ronald McDonald for the McDonald's Corporation. My marketplace covered most of Arizona and a portion of Southern California.

One of our standard events was "Ronald Day." One day each month, we visited as many of the community hospitals as possible, bringing a little happiness into a place where no one ever looks forward to going. I was very proud to be able to make a difference for children and adults who were experiencing some "down time." The warmth and gratification I would receive stayed with me for weeks. I loved the project, McDonald's loved the project, the kids and adults loved it and so did the nursing and hospital staffs.

There were two restrictions placed on me during a visit. First, I could not go anywhere in the hospital without McDonald's personnel (my handlers) as well as hospital personnel. That way, if I were to walk into a room and frighten a child, there was someone there to address the issue immediately. And second, I could not physically touch anyone within the hospital. They did not want me transferring germs from one patient to another. I understood why they had this "don't touch" rule, but I didn't like it. I believe that touching is the most honest form of communication we will ever know. Printed and spoken words can lie; it is impossible to lie with a warm hug.

Breaking either of these rules, I was told, meant I could lose my job.

Toward the end of my fourth year of "Ronald Days," as I was heading down a hallway after a long day in grease paint and on my way home, I heard a little voice. "Ronald, Ronald."

I stopped. The soft little voice was coming through a half-opened door. I pushed the door open and saw a young boy, about five years old, lying in his dad's arms, hooked up to more medical equipment than I had ever seen. Mom was on the other side, along with Grandma, Grandpa and a nurse tending to the equipment.

I knew by the feeling in the room that the situation was grave. I asked the little boy his name—he told me it was Billy—and I did a few simple magic tricks for him. As I stepped back to say good-bye, I asked Billy if there was anything else I could do for him.

"Ronald, would you hold me?"

Such a simple request. But what ran through my mind was that if I touched him, I could lose my job. So I told Billy I could not do that right now, but I suggested that he and I color a picture. Upon completing a wonderful piece of art that we were both very proud of, Billy again asked me to hold him. By this time my heart was screaming "yes!" But my mind was screaming louder. "No! You are going to lose your job!"

This second time that Billy asked me, I had to ponder why I could not grant the simple request of a little boy who probably would not be going home. I asked myself why was I being logically and emotionally torn apart by someone I had never seen before and probably would never see again.

"Hold me." It was such a simple request, and yet . . .

I searched for any reasonable response that would allow me to leave. I could not come up with a single one. It took me a moment to realize that in this situation, losing my job may not be the disaster I feared.

Was losing my job the worst thing in the world?

Did I have enough self-belief that if I did lose my job, I would be able to pick up and start again? The answer was a loud, bold, affirming "yes!" I could pick up and start again.

So what was the risk?

Just that if I lost my job, it probably would not be long before I would lose first my car, then my home . . . and to be honest with you, I really liked those things. But I realized that at the end of my life, the car would have no value and neither would the house. The only things that had steadfast value were experiences. Once I reminded myself that the real reason I was there was to bring a little happiness to an unhappy environment, I realized that I really faced no risk at all.

I sent Mom, Dad, Grandma and Grandpa out of the room, and my two McDonald's escorts out to the van. The nurse tending the medical equipment stayed, but Billy asked her to stand and face the corner. Then I picked up this little wonder of a human being. He was so frail and so scared. We laughed and cried for 45 minutes, and talked about the things that worried him.

Billy was afraid that his little brother might get lost coming home from kindergarten next year, without Billy to show him the way. He worried that his dog wouldn't get another bone because Billy had hidden the bones in the house before going back to the hospital, and now he couldn't remember where he put them.

These are problems to a little boy who knows he is not going home.

On my way out of the room, with tear-streaked makeup running down my neck, I gave Mom and Dad my real name and phone number (another automatic dismissal for a Ronald McDonald, but I figured that I was gone and had nothing to lose), and said if there was anything the McDonald's Corporation or I could do, to give me a call and consider it done. Less than 48 hours later, I received a phone call from Billy's mom. She informed me that Billy had passed away. She and her husband simply wanted to thank me for making a difference in their little boy's life.

Billy's mom told me that shortly after I left the room, Billy looked at her and said, "Momma, I don't care anymore if I see Santa this year because I was held by Ronald McDonald."

Sometimes we must do what is right for the moment, regardless of the perceived risk. Only experiences have value, and the one biggest reason people limit their experiences is because of the risk involved.

For the record, McDonald's did find out about Billy and me, but given the circumstances, permitted me to retain my job. I continued as Ronald for another year before leaving the corporation to share the story of Billy and how important it is to take risks.

Jeff McMullen

"If I Were Really Important . . ."

No one ever finds life worth living—he has to make it worth living.

Author unknown

In one of my "Dare to Connect" workshops, I instructed all my students to participate full-out in their jobs for one entire week. I asked them to "act as if" their actions really made a difference to everyone around them. The key question they were to ask themselves during the week was:

"If I were really important here,
what would I be doing?"

And then they were to set about doing it.

Peggy resisted the assignment. She lamented that she hated her job in a public relations firm and was just biding her time until she found a new one. Each day was pure drudgery as she watched the clock slowly move through eight painful hours. With great skepticism, she finally agreed to try it for just one week—to commit 100 percent to her job, "as if" she really counted.

The following week, as I watched Peggy walk into the room, I couldn't believe the difference in her energy level. With excitement in her voice, she reported the events of her week.

"My first step was to brighten up the dismal office with some plants and posters. I then started to really pay attention to the people I work with. If someone seemed unhappy, I asked if there was anything wrong and if I could help. If I went out for coffee, I always asked if there was anything I could bring back for the others. I complimented people. I invited two people for lunch. I told the boss something wonderful about one of my co-workers (usually, I'm selling myself!)."

Then Peggy asked herself how she could improve things for the company itself. "First, I stopped complaining about the job—I realized I was such a nag! I became a self-starter and came up with a few very good ideas that I began implementing." Every day, she made a list of things she wanted to accomplish and set about accomplishing them. "I was really surprised by how much I could do in a day when I focused on what I was doing!" she said. "I also noticed how fast the day goes when I am involved. I put a sign on my desk that said, 'If I were really important here, what would I be doing?' And every time I started to fall back into my old patterns of boredom and complaining, the sign reminded me what I was supposed to be doing. That really helped."

What a difference a simple question made in just one short week! It made Peggy feel connected to everyone and everything around her—including the organization itself. And whether Peggy chose to stay in her current job or not, she had learned a way to transform any work experience.

Susan Jeffers, Ph.D.

That One Moment

You have to do it by yourself,
and you can't do it alone.

Martin Rutte

My mother is a teacher, and I grew up with the struggles and challenges a teacher faces. I often asked her, "Why do you teach? How can you continue to put out the kind of energy you do?" The answer was always the same. "There is always that one child, that one moment that makes it all worthwhile."

I'm not sure if it was heredity, my mother's inspiration, or the heartfelt stories she would share about her students, but I, too, became a teacher. However, my classroom is quite different from hers. I do my teaching outdoors. I teach adventure-based education, physically and mentally challenging activities that involve some risk and that focus on pro-social development. Most of the work I do involves at-risk youths.

When my mother asked me why I taught, how I was able to overcome such hardships, I knew that she already had the answer. As she said, it's that one child, that one special moment.

One of those moments happened recently. I was working with a group of female youths between the ages of 12 and 15. We were nearing the end of the second week of a four-week program. The group had progressed smoothly through the "Team" elements and was moving to a "High" element called the Wire Walk.

The Wire Walk involves climbing up a pegged tree to a wire cable, 25 feet off the ground, stepping onto the wire cable, then walking across the cable, holding on to a loosely tied rope five feet above. During the entire process, from ground to finish, the participant is attached to one end of a climbing rope for safety. The other end is controlled by a trained instructor. It is a very safe procedure.

We spent some time talking about the emotions the girls had, then I asked who was willing to try. A few girls raised their hands, and they were able to complete the Wire Walk with little difficulty. Once the other girls saw their success, a few more were ready to go.

"Who would like to go next?" I asked. A few of the girls said, "Susie's ready." Sensing her reluctance, I asked Susie if she was ready. She answered softly, "I suppose."

Susie was safely tied in and standing at the foot of the tree. I took up the slack in the rope as I watched her make the long reach for the first peg. The group applauded her efforts with rally cries and cheers. Then I watched Susie's face tighten with every step. I wanted so much for her to do the Wire Walk. I knew how good it would make her feel. But I'd seen this fear many times, and I realized she would not go much farther.

She was halfway up when she embraced the tree in a big hug—the kind of hug a small child gives a parent's leg after being frightened. Her eyes were shut tight, her knuckles white. With her cheek pressed against the bark, all I heard was, "I can't."

The other girls sat in silence. I began to quietly talk to Susie, trying to get her to ease her grip enough to lower her down. I talked for what seemed a long time. Then I ran out of words and was quiet.

The silence was broken by Mary. "I will be your friend no matter what, Susie!"

My eyes filled with tears, so much so that I could barely see Susie clinging to the tree. By the time my eyes cleared, I saw that she had lifted her head to look up to the wire. The white in her knuckles had gone flush. She turned to look down at Mary and smiled. Mary smiled back. I was on the job again, taking up the slack in the rope until Susie reached the wire.

Moments like this keep me doing what I do. The young hearts that I work with continue to fill me with inspiration and courage. I truly believe their lives are filled with more choices of risk and danger than I ever had. Somehow they go on. Somehow they get to the wire.

As for Susie, she made it all the way across that wire. When she returned to the ground, the first hug she looked for was from Mary.

We all cheered.

Chris Cavert

A Little Courage Goes a Long Way

What lies behind us and what lies before us are tiny matters compared to what lies within us.

Ralph Waldo Emerson

It was 1986. I had just closed my advertising agency and was close to broke, with no idea as to what to do next. Then one day, after reading a magazine article that talked about the power of networking, a light bulb went off. These were the 1980s. Why weren't people making money networking? As I began to question, the idea came: I would create a company called POWERLUNCH! People seeking contacts would call me, and in the role of business *yenta* (matchmaker), I would, over the computer, find the exact type of person in the industry they needed, or the exact position they were looking for. Then I'd put the right people together for a power lunch. Perfect, right?

The only problem was that I had very little money to start a business, so I used the one asset that has never failed me—my mouth. I printed 10,000 brochures at an inexpensive local print shop, got up my courage and planted myself on the corner of Connecticut and K Avenues in the middle of downtown Washington, D.C. At the top of my lungs I yelled, "POWERLUNCH! Get your POWERLUNCH!" For three days, I yelled and passed out brochures. People looked at me a little funny, but they took them.

At the end of three days, all the brochures were gone and not one person had called. Penniless, lifeless and beginning to lose hope, I dragged myself home. As I walked in the door, the telephone rang. It was a *Washington Post* reporter. He had seen one of my brochures and wondered if he could interview me to be on the front page of the *Post's* "Style" section. Now, mind you, I had no company, no business phone (he called me on my personal line), and not much of a structure for my business—but I excitedly agreed.

The next day we had a great interview, and he asked me for my business phone number. I told him I would get back to him with it that afternoon. I then scrambled down to the local phone company and called him with the number: 265-EATT. (It hadn't been hooked up yet, but at least I had a number.) Amused, the reporter agreed to print it— a rarity for the *Post.*

The next day I was awakened by a phone call—on my personal line—from a friend congratulating me on the article in the paper. I sat bolt upright in bed. But my new phone number hadn't been hooked up yet! Just then, there was a knock on the door. It was the woman from the telephone company, thank goodness, come to hook me up. She went to the back of the house and emerged after about 15 minutes with a piece of paper. "What's this?" I asked.

"These are the messages I took while I was on the pole," she replied with a laugh. My business was already one step ahead of me.

From there, many other media sources called, including the *New York Times*, the *Christian Science Monitor* and even *Entertainment Tonight*. I received hundreds of requests for lunches and introduced many people. I was able to fulfill my desire to have fun and do business at the same time. And it all started on the corner of Connecticut and K, with a lot of yelling . . . and a little bit of courage.

Sandra Crowe

"This, Caldwell, is the ultimate in power lunches!"

Reprinted with permission from Dave Carpenter.

It Takes Chutzpah!

*To dare is to lose one's footing momentarily.
To not dare is to lose oneself.*

Søren Kierkegaard

Shortly after I began a career in business, I learned that Carl Weatherup, president of PepsiCo, was speaking at the University of Colorado. I tracked down the person handling his schedule and managed to get myself an appointment. I was told, however, that he was on a tight schedule and only had a 15-minute block available after his talk to the business class.

So there I was, sitting outside the university's auditorium, waiting for the president of PepsiCo. I could hear him talking to the students . . . and talking, and talking. I became alarmed: his talk wasn't ending when it should have. He was now five minutes over, which dropped my time with him down to 10 minutes. Decision time.

I wrote a note on the back of my business card, reminding him that he had a meeting. "You have a meeting with Jeff Hoye at 2:30 P.M." I took a deep breath, pushed open the doors of the auditorium and walked straight up the middle aisle toward him as he talked. Mr. Weatherup stopped, I handed him the card, then I turned and walked out the way I came. Just before I reached the door, I heard him tell the group that he was running late. He thanked them for their attention, wished them luck and walked out to where I was now sitting, holding my breath.

He looked at the card and then at me. "Let me guess," he said. "You're Jeff." He smiled. I began breathing again and we grabbed an office right there at school and closed the door.

He spent the next 30 minutes offering me his time, some wonderful stories that I still use, and an invitation to visit him and his group in New York. But what he gave me that I value the most was the encouragement to continue to do as I had done. He said that it took nerve for me to interrupt him, and that the business world or anywhere else was all about nerve. When things need to happen, you either have the nerve to act or you don't.

Jeff Hoye

A Captive Audience

Your future depends on many things, but mostly on you.

Frank Tyger

On my way out of town and in a hurry, I hailed a taxi in front of my apartment building at 64th and 1st in Manhattan. "Kennedy Airport," I instructed the driver.

When I was settled comfortably in the back seat, an unusually friendly New York cab driver started a conversation with me.

"Nice apartment building you live in," he said.

"Yes," I replied, distractedly.

"Live there very long?"

"No."

"I bet you must have a really small closet there," he said.

Now he had my attention. "Yes," I said, "quite small."

"Have you ever heard of closet organizers?" he asked.

"Yes, I guess I've seen an ad or something in the newspapers."

"I only drive a cab part-time," he said. "My full-time job is organizing people's closets. I come in and put shelves and drawers and this and that in closets."

Then he asked me if I had ever considered having my closet organized.

"Well, I don't know," I said. "I do need some extra closet space. Isn't there another closet company out there, California something?"

"You mean California Closet Company. They're the really big company in the business. I can do exactly what they can do but for less money."

"Oh, really?"

"Yeah," he said. And with this, the driver gave me a detailed explanation of what a professional closet organizer does. He finished by saying, "When you call up California Closet and they come to your house to make an estimate, this is what you do: Ask them to leave you a copy of the plans. Now, they won't want to leave you anything, but if you tell them you need it to show your girlfriend or wife, they'll give you a copy. Then you call me, and I'll do the same thing—but for 30 percent less money."

"That sounds very interesting," I said. "Here, let me give you my business card, and if you call me at my office, we'll set up a meeting."

I handed him my card and he nearly swerved off the road.

"Oh, my God," he shouted, "you're Neil Balter! You're the founder of California Closet. I saw you on the 'Oprah Winfrey Show,' and I thought you had such a good idea, I went into business myself."

He looked in the rear-view mirror and studied me. "I should have recognized you. Gosh, Mr. Balter, I apologize. I didn't mean you guys were an expensive company. I didn't mean . . ."

"Calm down," I said. "I like your style. You're a pretty smart fellow and you're aggressive. I admire that. You have a captive audience in your cab, and you took advantage of it. It takes chutzpah to do what you do. Why don't you call me, and we'll see what we can do about having you become one of our salesmen?"

Needless to say, he came to work for us—and became one of California Closet's top salespeople!

Neil Balter

BIZARRO

By DAN PIRARO

The "Bizarro" cartoon by Dan Piraro is reprinted courtesy Chronicle Features, San Francisco, California.

A True Leader

The time is always right to do what is right.

Martin Luther King Jr.

A few years ago, Pioneer Hi-Bred International, where I was employed, purchased Norand Corporation. Pioneer's sales representatives in the field used Norand hand-held terminals to upload daily sales information and download new price and sales incentive information. Pioneer bought so many of these hand-held terminals, the economics made the purchase of Norand look interesting. Owning Norand also allowed Pioneer to explore high-technology markets outside agriculture.

But after a few years, the emerging laptop PC technology made the hand-held units obsolete. Pioneer sold Norand at a loss. Pioneer always took a given percent of the annual profits to divide equally among all employees, so our profit-sharing checks were lower than if Pioneer had not purchased Norand. Additionally, my Pioneer stock was lower than it had been before the purchase of Norand. I was not pleased.

The CEO of Pioneer, Tom Urban, made annual formal visits to each of the Pioneer divisions to talk about the state of the business and to listen to employees' concerns. When he walked into the meeting room for his first visit after the sale of Norand, he acknowledged the group, removed his jacket and neatly folded it across the back of the chair. He loosened his tie, undid his collar and rolled up his sleeves. The next thing he said was the last thing I ever expected to hear a CEO say.

He said, "I made a mistake buying Norand and I am sorry. I am sorry your profit-sharing was lower because of the purchase, and I am sorry your stock was hurt by the purchase. I will continue to take risks, but I am a bit smarter now, and I will work harder for you." The room was quiet for a moment before he asked for questions.

A great man and leader stood before us that day. As I sat listening to him, I knew I could trust him, and that he deserved every bit of loyalty I could give to him and to Pioneer. I also knew I could take risks in my own job.

In the brief moment of silence before the questions started, I recall thinking that I would follow him into any battle.

Martin L. Johnson

The Scoutmaster and the Gunslinger

Our mission is to gain true discernment of the contraries, first as contraries, but then as poles of unity.

Hermann Hesse

When the two top people at the helm of the large insurance company realized that their inability to work together was a problem—not just for them, but for the whole organization—it was almost too late. They found themselves at that point best described in nautical terms as being in extremism. That's when only radical, correct and immediate action by both ships will avoid a collision. I was doing some intensive leadership training for their company when they asked for help. Here's what happened:

The chief executive officer, Brad, had this to say about his chief operating officer, Miles: "The guy's headstrong. Out of control. Always going off half-cocked and doing stuff we have to bail ourselves out of. It's scary for me to even think about letting him get close to the budget. If he were in charge, we'd never be able to do the same thing twice in a row. We'd be jumping off cliffs and figuring out what to do on the way down. Drives me crazy! See if you can fix him, please . . ."

Meanwhile surprise, surprise—Miles, the chief operating officer, was having a tough time with Brad. "He's s-o s-l-o-w to take action. I get cobwebs on the proposals I make before he even reads them. He always has 16 reasons why we can't do it, and by the time we get him on board, the moment has passed us by. Drives me crazy! Get him off my back, please."

Although they were able to conduct themselves in a professional manner in public and maintained a thin veneer of friendliness, the strains between them had leaked down and out to the rest of the company—in some cases, aided and abetted by their own gossip. As a result, staff were forced to take sides. "Are you with Brad or are you with Miles?"

After a brief conversation with each of them, they agreed that it was time to bury the hatchet and asked for some assistance. "Let's go off in a room at a nearby conference center and lock the door until this thing gets resolved," I suggested.

They both came into the room smiling but a little nervous. "Okay," I said, "first of all, you have to understand the huge negative impact your unresolved stuff is having on your company. You have each lost a lot of respect out there, even from the people who agree with you. The two of you both think—although you would never say it out loud—that the only solution is to have one of you go away, and you are each plotting how that might be expedited.

"Here's the truth as I see it," I continued. "Unless you find a way to regain mutual trust and respect, this whole company is in jeopardy. Are you willing to pursue that goal?"

They both said yes. "How do we do it?"

"First, you need to understand that each of you represents not a problem to be solved, but one end of a polarity that must be managed. Let's take a few minutes to discover how that plays out with the two of you."

In the next hour, Brad found out that he had been trying all his life to be a good person. He had, in fact, been a national leader in the Boy Scouts. His highest values were tied to dependability, consistency, preparation, caution and responsibility. Miles, on the other hand, had grown up getting his rewards from being creative, innovative, quick, energetic, light-hearted and inspirational.

Using an approach adapted from Barry Johnson, author of *Polarity Management,* I invited each of them to give his way of operating a name, based on some character from literature or history. Brad said, "Mine's easy! It's got to be the Scoutmaster! I've been trying to be better than Miles and showing him how he should be doing things. It's my job as the Scoutmaster to keep everybody- especially Miles—headed in the right direction and out of trouble."

"Yeah, I can see that," said Miles. "How about this for me. the Gunslinger? I'm quick on the trigger, too quick a lot of the time. Impulsive. That leads to a certain amount of chaos, which is fine for me and a few others, but wreaks havoc on the organization. I've been subtly trying to show Brad up, make him look slow and out-of-date."

This was a moment of truth. They would either rise to the necessary levels of courage, authenticity and leadership or slide back into their self-protective patterns. Bless their hearts, they both stepped into the abyss, let go and reached for something heretofore unseen and unknown.

"I'm sorry, Miles, that I've been such a know-it-all with you and made you wrong so often. I especially apologize for gossiping about you to your peers."

"Me, too, Brad. I'm sorry that I've been so hard to get along with, showing you up with my sarcastic jokes and smirking at you behind your back to my buddies."

The forgiveness that was needed was released by each of them to the other, along with a few tears of relief and joy. This was a holy moment. Electricity in the air. Hearts beating faster. They hugged each other.

After a few minutes, it was time to move it to the organizational level. I suggested that what was needed was an organization that had mastered *both* of these ways of operating; that if either of them had somehow "won" the fight and managed to impose his particular way of operating on the whole organization, that the company would have been in big trouble fast.

They agreed to shift their efforts from trying to defeat the other person to actually supporting him, looking for ways to strengthen him, making him more powerful, more effective. They predicted ways they would sabotage this agreement and determined what they would do when that happened. They both pledged to stop gossiping as of that moment and agreed to meet regularly for the next three months to keep tabs on how they were doing.

Talk about courage. The next day they called a meeting of the senior leadership team. Brad went in wearing his big Scoutmaster's hat, Miles wearing a cowboy hat and a set of his eight-year-old son's six-guns. Slowly and carefully, the two of them walked the group through their whole interaction, taking time to explain in detail the most embarrassing stuff. The group was astounded. They laughed together. They cried a little. They gave them a standing ovation at the end. The results were instantaneous and striking.

Customers noticed the difference. The most prescient of all indicators, the executive secretaries, noticed the difference. Their wives noticed. The other officers in the holding company noticed. They have worked through several conflicts since then that, by their admission, would have stopped the wagon before. And miraculously, Brad, the uptight Boy Scout, has loosened up to the point that he brought the house down at a recent employee gathering. Miles, meanwhile, has been given—and is taking—responsibility for the budget.

The most amazing outcome of this example of courage and leadership occurred last week when Brad gathered his leadership team and announced, "This is my last year here. I'll be retiring at the end of next year. I know you have been wondering who I would be recommending to the board for my replacement as CEO. I am delighted and somewhat surprised to say that it will be Miles. And it is with a real sense of confidence and optimism that I do this, knowing that he has what it takes to lead this company into the future."

It's amazing what a little courage in the right place at the right time can accomplish.

John Scherer

Showdown at Pebble Beach

Integrity is not a 90 percent thing, not a 95 percent thing; either you have it or you don't.

Peter Scotese

Back in the 1960s, in the early days of our company, I had a lesson that still strikes me as valuable. In those years, IMG's main involvement was with golf, and we were fortunate in having as clients both Arnold Palmer and Gary Player. Aside from being superlative athletes, Arnold and Gary were highly poised, attractive and utterly professional; they were constantly in demand and it was a great pleasure to handle their business.

At some point we were asked to arrange a deal between the Lincoln-Mercury division of the Ford Motor Company, as sponsors, and the Revue Studios, subsidiary of MCA, as producers, to do a series of shows called *Challenge Golf,* in which Palmer and Player would compete against other two-man teams.

The negotiations were highly amiable, and a contract was soon signed that provided, among other things, that the matches would be filmed during a 90-day period at various golf courses within California. In the course of the discussions, some specific venues had been talked about, but in the spirit of reason and cooperation that then prevailed, there seemed no need to spell them out in the written agreement.

The plot thickened, however, when the bean counters from Revue sat down with their adding machines and figured out that the studio could save a fair amount of money by filming all the matches on courses in and around Los Angeles. There would be less overtime to pay, and no travel or lodging expenses for crews and production executives. So Revue's lawyers scoured the contract, and—what do you know?—there was nothing in it that said the matches *couldn't* all be played right there in Los Angeles and Orange Counties.

There was only one small problem. Lincoln-Mercury's general manager, Chase Morsey, remembered quite specifically that during the negotiations it had been clearly understood that some of the matches would take place in northern California. In fact, one in particular would be played at Pebble Beach—a glamorous and upscale club with which Lincoln-Mercury wanted, understandably, to be associated.

So Morsey got *his* lawyers on the case, trying to find something in the contract that gave Lincoln-Mercury the right of approval on the choice of courses, or, if need be, to tank the agreement altogether.

By this point everyone was getting mad at each other, and a deal that had begun as a love feast was giving everybody headaches. As it turned out, however, the stalemate was easily broken by a single phone call from Morsey to Lew Wasserman, the chairman of MCA.

Morsey told Wasserman his side of the story, and Wasserman, in turn, confronted his people with a single question: "Did you or did you not lead the executives of Lincoln-Mercury to believe there would be a show produced at Pebble Beach?"

He didn't want to know what the contract said. He didn't want to know about his company's legal rights. He didn't want to hear about what the change in venue would cost.

He just wanted an answer to that simple question.

When MCA's people acknowledged that there *had,* in fact, been talk about a match at Pebble Beach, Wasserman told them to apologize to Morsey, dispatch a crew to Carmel pronto, and stop wasting everybody's time.

In that single exchange, Morsey and Wasserman not only got *Challenge Golf* back on track, but cemented the relationship between their two companies by making it clear that each would stand by its commitments— whether or not those commitments were expressed in letter-perfect legal form.

Mark H. McCormack

Take a Stand

One individual plus courage is a majority.

Source Unknown

Jackie Robinson made history when he became the first black baseball player to break into the major leagues by joining the Brooklyn Dodgers. Branch Rickey, owner of the Dodgers at that time, told Robinson, "It'll be tough. You're going to take abuse you never dreamed of. But if you're willing to try, I'll back you all the way."

And Rickey was right. Jackie was abused verbally (not to mention physically by runners coming into second base). Racial slurs from the crowd and members of his own team, as well as from opponents, were standard fare.

One day, Robinson was having it particularly tough. He had booted two ground balls, and the boos were cascading over the diamond. In full view of thousands of spectators, Pee Wee Reese, the team captain and Dodger shortstop, walked over and put his arm around Jackie right in the middle of the game.

"That may have saved my career," Robinson reflected later. "Pee Wee made me feel that I belonged."

Be sure that the employees on your team feel that they belong.

Denis Waitley

9

LESSONS & INSIGHTS

Live to learn and you will learn to live.

Portuguese proverb

My rates: $200 for truths, $100 for insights, $10 for wisecracks.

Reprinted with permission from Harley Schwadron.

The Blind Man

Growth means change and change involves risks, stepping from the known to the unknown.
George Shinn

Buses, trains, airplanes and airports offer a safe haven for strangers to divulge intimate stories, knowing that they will probably never see one another again. Such was the case on this day in the spring of 1983 at La Guardia Airport. I was waiting for my plane when a tall, strong, handsomely tailored gentleman felt safe enough in his anonymity to sit next to me and share the following story:

"I was finishing up my work at my office in downtown Manhattan. My secretary had left about a half hour before, and I was just getting ready to pack up for the day when the phone rang. It's Ruth, my secretary. She's in a panic. 'I've left an important package on my desk by mistake. It needs to be immediately delivered to the Blind Institute. It's only a few blocks away. Could you help me out?'

"'You caught me at a good time; I was just walking out the door. Sure. I'll drop the package off for you.'

"As I walked into the Blind Institute, a man ran toward me. 'Thank heaven you arrived. We must get started at once.' He pointed to an empty chair next to him and told me to sit down. Before I could say anything, I was sitting in a row of people who were all sighted. Directly facing us was a row of sightless men and women. A young man, about 25 years old, stood in front of the room. He began giving us instructions.

"'In a moment, I will ask those of you who are sightless to get to know the person seated across from you. It will be important for you to take whatever time you need to distinguish their features, hair texture, bone type, rate of breathing and so forth. When I say 'begin,' you will reach across and touch the person's head, feel the texture of their hair, note if it is curly, straight, coarse or thin. Imagine what color it might be. Then slowly place your fingers on their brow. Feel the strength, the size, the texture of the skin. Use both hands to investigate the eyebrows, eyes, nose, cheekbones, lips, chin and neck. Listen to the person's breathing. Is it calm or rapid? Can you hear the heart beating? Is it fast or slow? Take your time—and now, begin.'

"I began to panic. I wanted out of this place. I don't allow anybody to touch me without my permission, let alone a man. He's touching my hair. God, this is uncomfortable. Now his hands are on my face; I'm perspiring. He'll hear my heart beating and know I'm panicking. Got to calm down, can't show him that I'm not in control. I felt a sigh of relief when it was finally over.

"'Next,' the young instructor continued, 'the sighted people will have the same opportunity to discover the person seated across from them. Close your eyes and imagine that you have never seen this person in your life. Decide what you want to know about this person. Who are they?

What are their thoughts? What kind of dreams might they have? Reach across and begin to touch their head. Feel the texture of their hair. What color is their hair?'

"His voice faded in the background. Before I could stop, I had my hand on the young man's head seated across from me. His hair felt dry and coarse. I couldn't remember the color of his hair. Hell, I never remembered the color of anybody's hair.

"In fact, I'd never really looked at anyone. I just told people what to do. People were dispensable to me—I never really cared about them. My business was important, the deals I made were important. This touching, feeling and knowing other people was definitely not me, nor would it ever be.

"I continued to touch the young man's eyebrows, nose, cheeks and chin. I felt myself weeping inside. There was a tenderness in my heart that I had not known, a vulnerability I never revealed to myself or anyone else around me. I felt it and was afraid. It was clear to me that I would be out of this building very soon. I would go and never come back.

"Dreams? Did this young man across from me have dreams? Why should I care? He's nothing to me. I've got two teenage kids—I don't even know their dreams. Besides, all they ever think of is cars, sports and girls. We don't talk much. I don't think they like me. I don't think I understand them. My wife—well, she does her thing and I do mine.

"I'm perspiring and breathing hard. The instructor tells us to stop. I put my hand down and sit back. 'Now,' he goes on, 'this is the last part of the exercise. You will each have three minutes to share with each other the experience you had getting to know your partner. Let your partner know what you were thinking and feeling. Tell them what you learned about them. The sightless person will go first.'

"My partner's name was Henry. He told me that at first he felt left out because he didn't think he was going to have a partner for the evening. He was glad I was able to make it on time. He went on to tell me that he felt I truly had courage to take the risks to emote and feel. 'I was impressed,' he explained, 'at the way you followed the instructions despite how resistant you were to them. Your heart is very lonely and very big. You want more love in your life but you don't know how to ask for it. I admire your willingness to discover the side of you that truly makes a difference. I know you wanted to bolt out of the room, but you stayed. I felt the same way when I first came here. But now I'm not as afraid of who I am anymore. It's okay for me to cry, feel afraid, panic, want to run, shut down from others, hide out in my work. These are just normal emotions that I am learning to accept and appreciate. You might want to spend more time down here and learn who you really are.'

"I looked across at this young sightless Henry and wept openly. I couldn't speak. There was nothing to say. I had never known a place like this in my entire life. I had never experienced this amount of unconditional love and wisdom. The only thing I remember saying to Henry was, 'Your hair is brown and your eyes are light.' He was probably the first person in my life whose eyes I would never forget. I was the blind man; it was Henry who had the vision to see who he was.

"It was time for the meeting to end. I picked up the envelope under my seat and brought it to the instructor. 'My secretary was supposed to drop this off to you earlier this evening. Sorry it got here late.'

"The instructor smiled and took the package, saying, 'This is the first time I have ever run an evening like this. I've been waiting for the instructions to arrive so I would know what to do. When they didn't, I just had to wing it.

I didn't realize you weren't one of the regular volunteers. Please accept my apologies.'

"I haven't told anyone, not even my secretary, that I go to the Blind Institute two nights each week. I can't explain it, but I actually think I'm starting to feel love for people. Don't tell anyone on Wall Street I said that. You know, it's a dog-eat-dog world and I have to stay on top of it—or do I? I don't seem to have answers to anything anymore.

"I know I've got a lot of learning to do if my sons are going to respect me. Funny, I've never said that before. Kids are supposed to respect their parents, or at least that's what I've always been told. Maybe it goes both ways. Maybe we can learn how to respect each other. For now, I'm beginning to learn how to respect and love myself."

Helice Bridges

How to Add by Subtracting

It takes 20 years to make an overnight success.

Eddie Cantor

There was a time when I constantly let my life get too cluttered. But a number of years ago, I stumbled on a good antidote for an overly complicated existence. Oddly enough, the answer came out of a business crisis, but I've been able to apply it to my personal life as well.

It happened in the winter of 1962. I was 29 then, with a wife and four children. I was working for a restaurant chain in Fort Wayne, Indiana. Four units that my boss had an interest in were in Columbus, Ohio, and they were in deep, deep trouble. My boss had even tried to sell them, but nobody was interested.

Something told me I could do something with them. Maybe I was being presumptuous, but by then I already had 17 years of experience in the food business. I was ambitious and full of ideas. Now, with this crisis in Columbus, I had a gut feeling that this could be my golden opportunity.

In early January, I went to Columbus to assess the situation. Business was bad; the management was worse. But there was one man who popped in there from time to time whom I really liked, a man I had known for a number of years. He was a colorful character from Kentucky who had an unusual recipe he'd created for fried chicken. His name was Harland Sanders and everybody called him the Colonel.

The Colonel had worked hard for many years, traveling around, selling franchises for his fried chicken to restaurants. He had a stake in our four failing restaurants. He was owed a lot of money, and if the restaurants failed, he'd be sure to lose it. But even he didn't want me to come.

I weighed the pros and cons, spent a long time praying about it and finally decided to go.

We owed everybody. Even the Colonel was obliged to make the deliveries of his secret blend of herbs and spices, C.O.D. Who could blame him? He didn't want to lose any more money.

I worked hard day and night, but there was no real improvement. I had the feeling the answer was right there under our noses, but I couldn't get a handle on it.

I'd walk around those restaurants hoping the answer would come leaping out at me. I'd survey row upon row of pickles, olives, catsup, soup. *It can't be that we're not well-stocked,* I'd think. Our menus took 10 minutes to read. We offered everything from baked beans to the Colonel's fried chicken.

I went down to a radio station in town to see about advertising. I cleared my throat and said to the manager, "Look . . . we're having a little cash flow problem right now. Do you think we could spread the payments out a bit?"

"I tell you what, Thomas," he said after a minute's reflection. "That fried chicken is the best thing you serve. I'll swap you some spots for some chicken."

Driving home, I was in a good mood for the first time in days. Praise God, we were making progress!

Suddenly it hit me so hard I almost swerved off the road—the Colonel's chicken!

Instead of driving home, I turned the car around and headed for one of the restaurants. I went straight to the pantry and jerked the pull-chain on the light. There they were: row upon row of pickles, olives, catsup, soup and everything else. Sure we had enough inventory—*we had too much!* We needed to simplify. We had to "accentuate the positive," and for us, the positive was Colonel Sanders' Kentucky Fried Chicken.

The more I thought about it, the more sense it made. If I sold all that expensive inventory, I'd have the cash I needed to buy chicken and the Colonel's herbs and spices. I'd be able to maintain high quality. I couldn't get over the simplicity. And yet it was in the simplicity that I was sure the strength of the idea lay.

Business picked up. In the weeks that followed, we changed our name to Colonel Sanders' Kentucky Fried Chicken Take-Homes. We sold chicken in buckets and barrels with the Colonel's beaming face on them. And business continued to build until the day came when I was able to hand the Colonel a check for the entire amount of our debt to him. The old man's hand trembled and he cried.

So there it was—an answer that anybody can apply in business or personal life. Simplify. Clear the shelves. Thin out the daily menu to make room for the things that really matter. Say no to the trivial; say yes to God.

When I began a restaurant of my own, I kept that principle in mind. I'd keep the menu simple. I'd have a little restaurant, I thought, with some Tiffany-style lamps and Brentwood chairs to go with my old-fashioned hamburgers. And I'd name my place after my daughter. I'd call it *Wendy's* ...

Dave Thomas

The Uncommon Professional

The only certain measure of success is to render more and better service than is expected of you.

Og Mandino

I went to the dark end of the inventory shelves, pressed my forehead against the wall and indulged myself in a few moments of quiet despair. Was this the way it would be for the rest of my life? Here I was, two years out of school, working at yet another mindless, low-pay, dead-end job. Up to this point, I had avoided the question by just not thinking about it, but now, for some reason, the awful possibility had come crashing down on me. The thought sucked every bit of energy from my body. I clocked out sick, went home to bed, pulled the covers over my head, and tried to forget about tomorrow and all the tomorrows that would follow.

By morning I was a little more composed, but no less depressed. Listlessly, I went back to work and resumed my hopeless drudgery.

There were several new guys on the job that morning—
temporary workers even lower on the totem pole than I
was. One of them caught my eye. He was older than the
others, and wearing a uniform. The company didn't issue
uniforms—in fact, the company didn't care what you
wore as long as you showed up. But this guy was decked
out in smartly pressed tan trousers and work shirt, complete with his name, Jim, embroidered on the pocket. I
guess he supplied himself with the uniform.

I watched him all that day and the rest of the days he
worked with us. He was never late or early. He worked at
a steady, unhurried pace. He was friendly to everyone he
worked with, but rarely talked while he was working. He
took the designated breaks at midmorning and afternoon
with everyone else, but unlike many others, he never lin-
gered past the allotted time.

At lunchtime, some of the crew brown-bagged it,
although most of us got our meals and drinks from the
vending machines. Jim didn't do either. He ate his lunch
from an old-fashioned steel lunch box and drank his coffee from a Thermos bottle—both of them well-worn with
use. Sometimes people would be a little careless about
cleaning up after they ate. Jim's place at the table was
spotless, and, of course, he was always back on the line
exactly on time. He wasn't just odd, he was outstanding—
admirable!

He was the kind of worker managers dream of. Despite
that, the other workers liked him, too. He didn't try to
show anybody up. He did what was asked of him, no
more, no less. He didn't gossip or complain or argue. He
just did the job—common labor—with more personal dignity than I had believed was possible with this kind of
low-level, grunt work.

His attitude and every action proclaimed that he was a
professional. Labor might be common; he wasn't.

When the temporary work was finished, Jim left for another job, but the impression he made on me didn't. Even though I had never talked to him, he turned my head completely around. I did the best I could to follow his example.

I didn't buy a lunch box or a uniform, but I did start setting my own standards. I worked like a businessman fulfilling a contract, just the way Jim had done. To my great surprise, the managers noticed my new productivity and promoted me. A few years later, I promoted myself to a better-paying job with a different company. And so it went. Eventually, many companies and many years later, I started a business of my own.

Whatever success I've had has been the result of hard work and good luck, but I think the biggest part of my luck was the lesson I learned from Jim so long ago. Respect doesn't come from the kind of work you do; it comes from the way you do the work.

Kenneth L. Shipley

Stressbusters

Therefore do not be anxious about tomorrow, for tomorrow will be anxious for itself. Let the day's own trouble be sufficient for the day.

Matthew 6:34

As a college freshman at Valparaiso University, facing all the uncertainties of future academic and work life, I had the opportunity to meet with the president emeritus and chancellor. Audiences were rare. Sitting among a small group of nervous peers, we anxiously awaited the arrival of a man revered throughout the school, let alone the country and abroad, for his excellence in achievement and esteemed wisdom.

Dr. O. P. Kretzman arrived in a wheelchair, aging, with failing sight. You could have heard a pin drop. All too soon, the attention turned to us as he asked for questions from the group. Silence. I knew inside what an opportunity this was, so despite my fear, I got up the courage to break the ice and ask my question.

"What advice would you give new freshman as we face

all the choices and uncertainties ahead of us?" His reply was simple and strong, "Take one bite out of the apple at a time." No more, no less. A perfect stressbuster for the moment and for all the moments of my life to come.

Now that I've been in the working world for 20 years, I've added a few more stressbusters to maintain a healthy life. Help yourself!

1. Change your priorities
2. Take stretch breaks
3. Step back and observe
4. Review your purpose
5. Get a massage
6. Leave five minutes earlier
7. See a comedy
8. Let go and let God!
9. Use affirmations
10. Organize your space
11. Share your feelings
12. Smell some flowers
13. Ask for acknowledg- ment
14. Listen to your intuition
15. Help someone else
16. Rub your feet and hands
17. Visualize positive out- comes
18. Take care of your health
19. Don't judge; bless
20. Work in the garden
21. Create a budget
22. Be empathetic, not overly sensitive
23. Be still and meditate
24. Use time-saving tech- nology
25. Carpool and enjoy the ride
26. Set aside time for plan- ning
27. Count your blessings
28. Don't forget, write it down
29. Simplify, simplify, sim- plify
30. Talk it out with co- workers
31. Eliminate destructive self-talk
32. Schedule play time
33. Change your environ- ment
34. Go with your natural rhythms
35. Find an easy place to give your gifts
36. Fully express yourself
37. View problems as opportunities
38. Let go of "what ifs"
39. Be clear what's expected of you
40. Ask the experts
41. Do your best and then stop

42. Trust Divine timing and order
43. Develop patience
44. Breathe deeply
45. Take a walk
46. Complete things
47. Take a nap
48. Sing a tune
49. Take a warm bath
50. Talk out your worries
51. Delegate
52. Talk with your mom or dad
53. Say no at times
54. Shift deadlines
55. Follow your passion
56. Tell a joke
57. Play out your fears
58. Drink lots of good water
59. Create a support sytem
60. Divide up big projects
61. Seek advice
62. Be gentle with yourself
63. Don't "enable" others
64. Pray for openings
65. Tell the truth
66. Get more restful sleep
67. Forgive and move on
68. Prepare food ahead
69. Fix it or get a new one
70. Be prepared to wait
71. Don't always be right
72. Focus on the moment
73. Take a lunch break
74. Read a book
75. Shift your attitude
76. Laugh each day
77. Develop self-esteem
78. Take vitamin supplements
79. Stop the "shoulds"
80. Avoid excess
81. Plan a special outing
82. See through illusions
83. Relax your muscles
84. Slow down and notice
85. Nurture good friends
86. Be in nature
87. Listen to music
88. Limit caffeine and sugar
89. Go on a fast or cleanse
90. Be spontaneous
91. Love your partner
92. Get some fresh air
93. Be pampered
94. Volunteer
95. Join help networks
96. Maintain good posture
97. Respect your limits
98. Exercise routinely
99. Go dancing
100. Sigh occasionally
101. Do yoga
102. Have a good cry
103. Make time for hobbies
104. Limit work time
105. Compromise/cooperate
106. Don't procrastinate
107. Unplug your phone/TV
108. Relax your standards
109. Journal your thoughts
110. Take a vacation
111. Organize your desk

112. Develop flexibility
113. Allow for imperfections
114. Don't overschedule
115. Expose your secrets
116. Build a strong body
117. Nurture your faith
118. Open a savings account
119. Take in the sun

120. Love and be loved
121. Get the facts
122. Work as a team
123. Smile—open your heart
124. Validate yourself
125. Daydream
126. Know God loves you!

Tim Clauss

"Take a break, Marvin! Take a break!!"

A Lesson in Leadership

It is not who is right, but what is right, that is of importance.

Thomas Huxley

I was born in South Africa, two years before apartheid was instituted as the political and social system of the land. I was raised with all the privileges of a white South African, and I was taught that the people with the greatest authority were also the people with the greatest competence. On my first job, one man dislodged me permanently from my mistaken belief.

At age 20, I left the white beaches of Cape Town, where I had been raised, to pursue a career in Johannesburg. "Egoli," the City of Gold, teemed with millions of tribal laborers. Like me, they came to the belly of South Africa to partake of its riches. They worked—often under extreme conditions and with bleak futures—to sustain their own bodies and their families hundreds of miles away in their homelands. I worked expecting that my sacrifices would pay off in perpetual promotion within the managerial class.

I worked in the factory. The plan called for me to spend several months in one department of the factory to learn how it functioned before being sent up to another department. In the end, I'd know the business from the ground floor up, and I'd be ready for the upper echelons of management.

In the first department, I—a novice—was expected to supervise eight experienced men. How could it be that a trainee was elevated to such responsibility? The answer in apartheid South Africa was a simple one: I was white and they were black.

Early one spring morning, I was summoned to the office of the managing director, Mr. Tangney. As I walked toward the plush administrative sanctums, I trembled. I knew what no one else had openly acknowledged. I was incompetent. For weeks, I had supervised the manufacture of precision brass water valves. Under my direction the crew produced an intolerably high percentage of scrap metal.

"Sit down, my boy," Mr. Tangney said. "I'm very pleased with the progress you're making, and I have a special job for you and your crew. You see, the summer hail this year is anticipated to be pretty bad again. Last year's hail damaged my car and the cars of the three other directors. We'd like you and your crew to construct a large carport to protect our cars."

"But sir," I stammered, "I don't know the first thing about construction!" Tangney seemed not to hear.

I did my best to figure out what materials were needed, ordered them, and we set to work. The men were uncharacteristically quiet as they did exactly what I told them. I instructed them to measure, saw and nail lumber together in several panels. I visualized the panels fitting together to form walls and a sturdy roof. Finally, the modules were constructed. It was time to fit everything together. I was anxious. The men were silent.

As the others looked on I helped one of the men, Philoman, set in place a heavy construction module. Philoman spoke very little English. Until that moment of cooperative effort, I had never made eye contact with him. Like most blacks in South Africa at that time—out of fear it would be considered a challenge—Philoman had learned to avert his eyes from the gaze of whites. As we maneuvered the heavy component into place, not having language to communicate, Philoman and I looked into one another's eyes and coordinated our movements. I will never forget his eyes. As our eyes locked, my identity as a supervisor fell away, and I saw not a black man struggling under a heavy load, but a co-worker.

But once again, my calculations were grossly off. Seeing my despondence at the ill-fitting construction, Philoman called to the others.

The crew all gathered around Philoman, talking and gesticulating excitedly. I got the feeling they were deciding my fate. Then Philoman took a stick and drew a rough diagram in the sand, talking all the while at the top of his lungs. Occasionally one of the others added something. Then, while I looked on helplessly, with Philoman directing, they proceeded to rectify the construction. After a few hours they were satisfied. Philoman called the crew and me together, and with a wide grin and sweat pouring down his face, he turned to me and said, "Basie, we fixed up."

I was grateful. I'll always treasure Philoman's lesson in leadership. But Philoman had done more for me than he intended. With great compassion and humility, he had shown me the truth of the apartheid system and the lie it perpetuated. Status has nothing to do with competence. A few months later I left that job, a far wiser young man.

Michael Shandler, Ed.D.

Mother Knows Best

We have 40 million reasons for failure, but not a single excuse.

Rudyard Kipling

During the early 1980s, I was a sales manager for a large training company. One of my responsibilities was to train people on how to sell. I was good at my job. I taught people that lack of time and opportunity were only tempting excuses for not producing results.

My mother, who lived near me, is a Greek immigrant from a family of 12. She has just a third-grade education. Her biggest hardship in coming to her new country was being separated from friends and relatives, some of whom came too; but they were living great distances away in our large city. The high point of each week was Sunday, when she would take an hour-long bus ride to church. Following the service, over a cup of Greek coffee, she and her friends would catch up and exchange gossip and stories of their families. She did this for 30 years.

The Greek population in our area grew sufficiently to

think about building a new church in our neighborhood. The committee members decided to raise the initial capital by selling raffle tickets. My mother jumped at the chance to participate. She had no formal training in the art of selling, but that never entered her mind. Her plan was simple: talk to as many people as possible about buying tickets and make them feel guilty if they didn't.

That's where I came into the picture. She said I was a big shot and that I must know a lot of people. She gave me 10 booklets of 10 tickets, each one worth one dollar, adding up to a grand total of $100. A week later, I showed up with only half of the tickets sold. Big mistake! "If only I had more time, I would have been able to sell all these tickets you gave me," I said to my mother. "I simply didn't have the time."

"What a load of baloney." (At least, it was the Greek equivalent of baloney.) "You either do something or you have all the excuses why not," my mother shot back. "You made time to go out to dinner, watch TV, jog, go to the movies. What does time have to do with it? Nothing! You think you're so smart with all your education and your important job, but you can't even tell the truth."

After that blast of the truth, she started to cry. I was devastated. I quickly agreed to buy the rest of my tickets myself. She stopped crying instantly and said, "When you want something, then you do whatever it takes to get the job done, even cry." With a smile she said, "I knew that crying would work with you, and for being so pathetic with your excuses, here are 10 more books. Now, go and sell them all." As a sales manager, I paled by comparison.

My mother went on to demonstrate that by not making excuses, she could produce outstanding results. She managed to out-sell every other volunteer, 14 to 1. She sold 7,000 tickets. Her closest challenge came from a neighbor who sold 500.

I learned a new level of distinction between time and results. I had always wanted to have my own business but had kept saying that it wasn't the right time and I didn't have the money. But I kept hearing my mother's voice in my mind: "You either do something that you want or you have all the reasons why you can't."

Six months later, I quit my job and started my own business, training people in time management. What other field could I possibly have chosen?

Nicholas Economou

Why Coaches Really Coach

Enthusiasm is the electric current that keeps the engine of life going at top speed . . .

B.C. Forbes

It was July. After a hard recruiting season and coming off a particularly tough playing season, it had been an unusually draining year. As head football coach at Canisius College in Buffalo, New York, I had taken on an almost impossible task two seasons previously: heading a football program where there had been no such program for over 25 years. After beating the bushes and visiting what seemed to be an endless array of high schools and student athletes' homes, I had assembled what was to be the finest group of incoming talent I had ever recruited.

Suddenly I was shaken from my self-imposed reflection. My secretary informed me that there was a young man who insisted on seeing me—not requesting, but insisting in a loud and pushy way. I asked her if he looked like a "football player" (big, mean and confident). "No, he looks like a guy who is coming to play, party and maybe study once in a while," she said.

I asked her to tell the boy I'd see him, find out what position he played and have him fill out our information form.

She returned within 30 seconds. "He's five-foot-eleven, 165 pounds and plays defensive end. He'll never make it." Both of our returning defensive ends were over 225 pounds. Each was over six feet three inches tall and had been a two-year starter.

As any college football coach will tell you, a good percentage of your time is taken up with "wanna-be" athletes who insist on playing until it is actually time to show up for practice. I braced myself for the usual drill. But there was no way to prepare myself for what was about to happen. Not only for the next 30 seconds . . . but for the rest of my life.

I got halfway out of my office when I was greeted by a veritable avalanche of enthusiasm.

"Hello, Coach Brooks. My name is Michael Gee. Spelled G-E-E. I'll bet you never heard of me. But you will. I guarantee it!"

I said, "You're right. I have no idea who you are or, frankly, why you're even here. We've finished our recruiting and we start practice in less than six weeks. Our roster is closed. I'm sorry, but . . ."

"Coach, I've researched it already. Football is a student activity. I've applied and been accepted as a freshman. I want to go out for the team. And you have to let me. I know the rules, Coach, but let me tell you why I can help you. I was a pre-season pick last year as an all-conference player. I started the season. I was always tired, always run down and I couldn't put much pressure on my leg. I went to the doctor. The news wasn't good. I had a malignant tumor in my thigh. But it's okay now, Coach. I promise.

Chemotherapy and rehabilitation have cleaned it up. I've even been working out. Coach, I know I can help you. I guarantee it! I can even run up to a mile without stopping."

I was really taken aback by all of this. My first response was to insist on a doctor's release. He gave it to me. I then asked if it was okay with his parents. He gave me a letter from them. He had me.

As it turned out, Michael Gee had me for the next four years. More correctly, I was lucky to have him. Three games into his freshman year, he was a starter. He led the team in sacks. He led the squad in tackles. Our inspirational leader, Michael became team captain. He even became an All-American! In addition, he was a dean's list student and active in every phase of campus life.

And Michael Gee savored life. When I was fortunate enough to win my 50th career victory, Mike Gee was the first player to congratulate me. When we beat our biggest rival, Mike Gee hoisted me to his shoulders. When we lost a tough game, Mike Gee was the first one to say, "Hey, Coach, it's just a game." Mike Gee was our son's first baby-sitter and the type of young man I hoped our son would become.

I often wonder what brought him into my life. I certainly don't have the answer. But I can tell you this. I learned a lot more from Mike Gee than I ever taught him, and that is a gift—the one that really does keep coaches coaching.

William T. Brooks

Let Your Light Shine

It's the essence of genius to make use of the simplest of ideas.

Charles Peguy

In a small town far away, a young man started his own business—a dime store at the corner of two streets. He was a good man. He was honest and friendly, and the people loved him. They bought his goods and they told their friends about him. His business grew and he expanded his store. In a matter of years, he developed his one store into a chain from coast to coast.

One day, he was taken ill to the hospital, and the doctors feared that his life was ending soon. He called together all three of his adult children and gave them this challenge: "One of the three of you will become the president of this company that I have built over the years. To decide which one of you deserves to become the president, I am going to give each of you a one-dollar bill. Go today and buy whatever you can with that one dollar, but when you get back here to my hospital room this evening, whatever you buy with your dollar must fill this room from corner to corner."

The children were all excited at the opportunity to run such a successful organization. Each went to town and spent the dollar. When they came back in the evening, the father asked, "Child number one, what have you done with your dollar?"

"Well, Dad," he said, "I went to my friend's farm, gave him my dollar, and bought two bales of hay." With that, the son went outside the room, brought in the bales of hay, undid them, and began to throw the hay up into the air. For a moment, the room was filled with hay. But in a few moments, the hay all settled on the floor and the room was not completely filled from corner to corner, as the father had instructed.

"Well, child number two, what have you done with your dollar?"

"I went to Sears," he said, "and bought two pillows made with feathers." He then brought in the pillows, opened them, and threw the feathers all over the room. In time, all the feathers settled down on the floor and the room was still not filled.

"And you, child number three," the father added, "what have you done with your dollar?"

"I took my dollar, Dad, and went to a store like the one you had years ago," the third child said. "I gave the owner my dollar and asked him for some change. Some quarters and dimes and nickels. I invested 50 cents of my dollar in something very worthwhile, just like the Bible says. Then I gave 20 cents of my dollar to two charitable organizations in our city. Twenty more cents I donated to our church. That left me with one dime. With the dime, I bought two items."

The son then reached in his pocket and took out a little matchbook and a little candle. He lit the candle, turned off the light switch, and the room was filled. From corner to corner, the room was filled—not with hay, not with feathers, but with light.

His father was delighted. "Well done, my son. You will become president of this company because you understand a very important lesson about life. You understand how to let your light shine. That is good."

Nido Qubein

Spiritual Unfoldment at the World Bank

I have learned this at least by my experiments: That if one advances confidently in the direction of his dreams, and endeavors to live the life which he has imagined, he will meet with a success unexpected in common hours.

Henry David Thoreau

Toward the end of 1992, I was nearing completion of the second draft of my book, *A Guide to Liberating Your Soul.* To get feedback, I invited about a dozen spiritually motivated colleagues from the World Bank to discuss the ideas and theories expressed in my book. We began a series of six brown-bag lunches.

A few weeks later, I accepted a challenging new job as assistant to one of the vice-presidents, and two colleagues from the brown-bag lunch group asked if I would set up a spiritual study group. Thinking I would be too busy, I asked for inner guidance—a sign from my soul.

A few days later, two women I didn't know called me

after reading a report about a seminar I had given in South Africa on "Liberating the Soul." They were also staff members and asked if I would set up some form of spiritual study group at the World Bank. I had little time to organize it, but they told me not to worry. "Just tell us what to do and we will do it." I had received my sign. That was the start of the Spiritual Unfoldment Society (SUS). Our purpose included:

- promoting personal transformation through self-knowledge and understanding, and awakening higher consciousness;
- providing a safe forum for the exchange of beliefs and ideas that promote spiritual awareness;
- encouraging the integration of higher consciousness into every aspect of our lives;
- seeking to create within the World Bank a consciousness of love and understanding that contributes toward transforming the way we interact with one another.

Within a matter of months after our first meeting, 40 to 50 people were attending. Although initially there was some fear about how colleagues might react to our society, it soon became perfectly respectable to be associated with the SUS.

A major boost to the Society came within a few months. The *Washington Post* featured the SUS in a magazine article. Management was particularly delighted with the following quote: "The World Bank, at 18th and H Streets NW, typically regarded as just another institutional pillar in the Washington power structure, is gaining a reputation for enlightenment." Soon we began getting calls from people who worked in the downtown area and who wanted to attend our weekly meetings.

Our membership grew to almost 400. We instituted monthly meditation sessions, created special-interest groups, held two retreats and published two newsletters. Members reported that the meetings had a profound impact on both their business and personal lives. We were feeding their souls.

From the steering committee also came the idea for an international conference to explore the link between spiritual values and sustainable development. After some initial hesitation, the World Bank agreed to sponsor the conference. The conference auditorium was packed with over 350 people from more than 20 countries. I heard people say, "I am totally amazed."

The outside world was finding it difficult to believe that this conservative monolith was holding a conference on ethical and spiritual values in relation to development. The real significance of the conference and of the Spiritual Unfoldment Society was that the Bank staff now have permission to talk about spiritual values in development, and to bring their hearts and souls to work.

Richard Barrett

It Is Later Than You Think

In 1938, I received a letter that completely changed my way of life:

Peking, China

Dear Doctor:

Please don't be too surprised in getting a letter from me. I am signing only my first name. My surname is the same as yours.

You won't even remember me. Two years ago I was in your hospital, under the care of another doctor. I lost my baby the day it was born.

That same day my doctor came in to see me, and as he left he said, "Oh, by the way, there is a doctor here with the same name as yours who noticed your name on the board, and asked me about you. He said he would like to come in to see you because you might be a relative. I told him you had lost your baby and I didn't think you would want to see anybody, but it was all right with me."

And then in a little while, you came in. You put your hand on my arm and sat down for a moment beside my bed. You didn't say much of anything, but your eyes

*and your voice were kind, and pretty soon I felt better.
As you sat there I noticed that you looked tired and that
the lines in your face were very deep. I never saw you
again but the nurses told me you were in the hospital
practically night and day.*

*This afternoon I was a guest in a beautiful Chinese
home here in Peking. The garden was enclosed by a
high wall, and on one side, surrounded by twining red
and white flowers, was a brass plate about two feet long.
I asked someone to translate the Chinese characters for
me. They said:*

Enjoy Yourself
It Is Later Than You Think

*I began to think about it for myself. I had not wanted
another baby because I was still grieving for the one I
lost. But I decided that moment that I should not wait
any longer. Perhaps it may be later than I think, too.
And then, because I was thinking of my baby, I thought
of you and the tired lines in your face, and the moment
of sympathy you gave me when I so needed it. I don't
know how old you are but I am quite sure you are old
enough to be my father; and I know that those few minutes you spent with me meant little or nothing to you,
of course—but they meant a great deal to a woman who
was desperately unhappy.*

*So I am so presumptuous as to think that in turn I
can do something for you, too. Perhaps for you it is later
than you think. Please forgive me, but when your work
is over, on the day you get my letter, please sit down
very quietly, all by yourself, and think about it.*

Marguerite

Usually I sleep very well when I am not disturbed by
the telephone, but that night I woke a dozen times, seeing

the brass plate in the Chinese wall. I dismissed the thing from my mind; but before I knew it I found myself saying again to myself: *Well, maybe it is later than you think; why don't you do something about it?*

I went to my office the next morning and told them I was going away for three months. Then I telephoned Shorty, my best friend, and asked him to come to my office. On his arrival I told him that I wanted him to go home and pack a grip and come on down to South America with me. I read him the letter. He shook his head. "I can't go," he said. "Of course I'd like to, but for weeks now I've been waiting to close a deal. I'm sorry, old man, but maybe sometime . . . sometime . . ." his words came more slowly. "What was that thing again that woman said? 'It is later than you think.' Well . . ."

He sat quietly for a moment. At last he spoke. "I waited three months for those people to make up their minds. I am not going to wait any longer. When would you like to go?"

We went to South America. By good fortune we were entertained by one of the prominent men of the country, a man who had built enormous steel plants and whose industries were growing rapidly.

During the visit Shorty asked our host if he played golf. He replied, "Señor, I play a little, I would like to play more. My wife is on vacation in the United States with our children. I would like to join her. I can do none of these things because I am too busy. I am 55 years old and in five years more I shall stop. It is true I said the same thing five years ago, but I did not know how much we should be growing. We are building a new plant."

"Señor," I said, "do you know why I am in South America?"

"Because," he said, "because perhaps you had not too much to do and had the necessary time and money to permit it."

"No," I replied, "I had a great deal to do and I did not have too much of either time or money."

I told him the story of the letter. Like Shorty, he made me repeat the words: "Enjoy yourself, it is later than you think." During the rest of the afternoon he seemed a bit preoccupied.

The next morning I met him in the corridor of our hotel. "Doctor," he said, "please wait a moment. I have not slept well. It is strange, is it not, that a casual acquaintance, which you would say yourself you are, could change the current of a very busy life. I have thought long and hard since I saw you yesterday. I have cabled my wife that I am coming."

He put his hand on my shoulder. "It was a very long finger indeed," he said, "that wrote those words on the garden wall in China."

Shorty, strong and well a few weeks ago, has gone to his reward. I spent the last hours at his bedside. Over and over again he said, "Fred, I am so happy that we went to South America together. I thank God we did not wait too long."

Frederic Loomis

How Much Is Enough?

The rich industrialist from the North was horrified to find the southern fisherman lying lazily beside his boat, smoking a pipe.

"Why aren't you out fishing?" said the industrialist.

"Because I have caught enough fish for the day," said the fisherman.

"Why don't you catch some more?"

"What would I do with them?"

"You could earn more money," was the industrialist's reply. "With that you could have a motor fixed to your boat and go into deeper waters and catch more fish. Then you would make enough to buy nylon nets. These would bring you more fish and more money. Soon you would have enough money to own two boats . . . maybe even a fleet of boats. Then you would be a rich man like me."

"What would I do then?" asked the fisherman.

"Then you could *really* enjoy life."

"What do you think I am doing right now?"

Anthony DeMello

More Chicken Soup?

Many of the stories that you have read in this book were submitted by readers like you as a response to our request for stories, or after having read the first three volumes of *Chicken Soup for the Soul*. We invite you, too, to share a story, poem or article that you feel belongs in a future volume of *Chicken Soup for the Soul at Work*. This may be a story you clip out of the local newspaper or that you find in a magazine, church bulletin or business newsletter. It may be something you read in a book or receive on the fax, that favorite quotation you have on the refrigerator door, a poem you have written or a personal experience that you believe will touch others.

In addition to future editions of *Chicken Soup for the Soul at Work*, we plan to publish other *Chicken Soup for the Soul* books every year. These include special collections of *Chicken Soup* for teachers, parents, salespeople, teenagers, athletes and animal lovers. We also plan to have a special volume of humorous stories, *Chicken Soup for the Laughing Soul*, as well as a collection of Christmas stories.

So let us hear from you. Please send a copy of your stories to:

Chicken Soup for the Soul
P.O. Box 30880 • Santa Barbara, CA 93130
fax: 805-563-2945 • e-mail: soup4soul@aol.com

We will be sure to credit both you and the author for your submission. Thank you for contributing to an upcoming batch of *Chicken Soup*.

Lectures, seminars and workshops

You may also contact us at the same address to schedule speaking engagements, or for information on our newsletters, other books, audiotapes, workshops and training programs.

Who Is Jack Canfield?

Jack Canfield is one of America's leading experts in the development of human potential and personal effectiveness. He is both a dynamic, entertaining speaker and a highly sought-after trainer. Jack has a wonderful ability to inform and inspire audiences toward increased levels of self-esteem and peak performance.

He is the author and narrator of several bestselling audio- and videocassette programs, including *Self-Esteem and Peak Performance, How to Build High Self-Esteem, Self-Esteem in the Classroom* and *Chicken Soup for the Soul—Live.* He is regularly seen on television shows such as *Good Morning America, 20/20* and *NBC Nightly News.* Jack has coauthored numerous books, including the *Chicken Soup for the Soul* series, *Dare to Win* and *The Aladdin Factor* (all with Mark Victor Hansen), *100 Ways to Build Self-Concept in the Classroom* (with Harold C. Wells) and *Heart at Work* (with Jacqueline Miller).

Jack is a regularly featured speaker at professional associations, school districts, government agencies, churches, hospitals, sales organizations and corporations. His clients have included the American Dental Association, the American Management Association, AT&T, Campbell Soup, Clairol, Domino's Pizza, GE, ITT, Hartford Insurance, Johnson & Johnson, the Million Dollar Roundtable, NCR, New England Telephone, Re/Max, Scott Paper, TRW and Virgin Records. Jack is also on the faculty of Income Builders International, a school for entrepreneurs.

Jack conducts an annual eight-day Training of Trainers program in the areas of self-esteem and peak performance. It attracts educators, counselors, parenting trainers, corporate trainers, professional speakers, ministers and others interested in developing their speaking and seminar-leading skills.

For further information about Jack's books, tapes and training programs, or to schedule him for a presentation, please contact:

The Canfield Training Group
P.O. Box 30880 • Santa Barbara, CA 93130
phone 800-237-8336 • fax 805-563-2945
website: http://www.chickensoup.com
to send e-mail: soup4soul@aol.com
to receive information via e-mail:
chickensoup@zoom.com

Who Is Mark Victor Hansen?

Mark Victor Hansen is a professional speaker who, in the last 20 years, has made over 4,000 presentations to more than 2 million people in 32 countries. His presentations cover sales excellence and strategies; personal empowerment and development; and how to triple your income and double your time off.

Mark has spent a lifetime dedicated to his mission of making a profound and positive difference in people's lives. Throughout his career, he has inspired hundreds of thousands of people to create a more powerful and purposeful future for themselves while stimulating the sale of billions of dollars worth of goods and services.

Mark is a prolific writer and has authored *Future Diary, How to Achieve Total Prosperity* and *The Miracle of Tithing.* He is coauthor of the *Chicken Soup for the Soul* series, *Dare to Win* and *The Aladdin Factor* (all with Jack Canfield) and *The Master Motivator* (with Joe Batten).

Mark has also produced a complete library of personal empowerment audio- and videocassette programs that have enabled his listeners to recognize and use their innate abilities in their business and personal lives. His message has made him a popular television and radio personality, with appearances on ABC, NBC, CBS, HBO, PBS and CNN. He has also appeared on the cover of numerous magazines, including *Success, Entrepreneur* and *Changes.*

Mark is a big man with a heart and spirit to match—an inspiration to all who seek to better themselves.

You can contact Mark at:

P.O. Box 7665
Newport Beach, CA 92658
phone 714-759-9304 or 800-433-2314
fax 714-722-6912

Who Is Maida Rogerson?

Born on Prince Edward Island, Canada, the setting for *Anne of Green Gables*, Maida Rogerson is an actor, singer and writer. Her distinguished 30-year career in theater and television has taken her from the Atlantic to the Pacific, and from northern Canada to Hollywood. Film and television credits include *Between Friends* with Elizabeth Taylor and Carol Burnett, and *Heartsounds* with Mary Tyler Moore and James Garner. She studied opera in Italy and has performed for Great Britain's Queen Elizabeth II.

Maida enjoys exploring a wide variety of artistic expression. She is an avid reader, with a special interest in cultural diversity and a deep appreciation for folk art, world music and ethnic dance. Her travels have taken her to the Orient, the Middle East, South America and Europe. Wherever she goes, Maida collects soulful stories and opens hearts to the richness and joy of living.

Since moving to the United States in 1990, Maida works with her husband, Martin Rutte, exploring the integration of spiritual values in the workplace. Her contributions to their company, Livelihood, include speechwriting, research and workshop development. From her home in Santa Fe, New Mexico, she continues her acting career and has completed two screenplays. Maida is currently researching two new books that deal with the power of acknowledgment and the use of order to simplify our lives.

Maida's work reflects a deep desire and commitment to help people open their hearts and experience the unity of all humankind. She believes that storytelling, whether through theater, books or other media, has the power to move, inspire and change us. You can contact Maida at:

Livelihood
64 Camerada Loop
Santa Fe, NM 87505
phone: 505-466-1510 • fax: 505-466-1514

Who Is Martin Rutte?

Martin Rutte is an international speaker and consultant. As president of Livelihood, a management consulting firm in Santa Fe, New Mexico, he explores the deeper meaning of work and its contribution to society. The company's focus includes strategic vision, corporate spirit and creative leadership.

Martin has worked with such organizations as Southern California Edison, Sony Pictures Entertainment, Labatt Breweries, the World Bank, Quad/Graphics, Virgin Records and London Life Insurance, helping them expand their outlook and position themselves for the future. He was the first Canadian to address the Corporate Leadership & Ethics Forum of The Harvard Business School, returning for four consecutive years as keynote speaker. He also twice addressed joint meetings of the American and Canadian Chambers of Commerce in Hong Kong.

A leader in the emerging management field of spirituality in the workplace, Martin is committed to reconnecting business with its natural source of creativity, innovation and compassion. His pioneering work on spirituality in the workplace was featured on the ABC-TV special, "Creativity: Touching the Divine." He was also the keynote presenter at the first International Conference on Spirituality in Business, held in Mazatlan, Mexico.

Articles on his innovative work have appeared in the *Miami Herald,* the *Toronto Star, South China Morning Post, Personnel Journal* and the *St. Louis Post-Dispatch.* He is currently working on a new book entitled *Being in Business: The Renaissance of Spirit at Work.*

Martin is a member of the board of advisors of Money Concepts Canada. He has served as a board member of Global Family and of The Hunger Project–Canada, and as a committee member of the Canadian Cancer Society. He enjoys monoprinting, international travel and networking with other innovative entrepreneurs.

For further information about Martin's speeches, tapes and consulting, please contact:

Livelihood
64 Camerada Loop
Santa Fe, NM 87505
phone: 505-466-1510 • fax: 505-466-1514

Who Is Tim Clauss?

Tim Clauss is a business educator, seminar leader and gifted spiritual counselor. As a private consultant focusing on intuitive knowing, Tim has supported thousands of people in achieving expanded results and more fulfilling lives. He is highly respected for his integrity, insight, sensitivity to situations and commitment to positive, uplifting shifts in people's lives.

Tim has been a professional organizer for 20 years, helping individuals and businesses to "bring order" and effectiveness to their environments. Clients have included corporations, hospitals, entrepreneurs, non-profit organizations, and a U.S. vice-presidential campaign, where he served as operations coordinator.

Tim also enjoys writing professionally. As vice president and seminar leader of a Chicago-based management firm, Tim coauthored trainings entitled *The Success Factor, Managing for Extraordinary Results,* and *Completing to Move On.* As part of Global Family, a non-profit peace organization represented in 40 countries, he coauthored *Social Creativity and Cooperation for the 1990s,* and continues to serve as advisor and editor of the organization's international newsletter.

Currently, Tim lives in northern New Mexico, where he is managing partner of the Taos Massage & Wellness Center. In addition to his consulting work, he enjoys teaching business at local natural healing schools. Tim's next book focuses on bringing order and simplicity to busy, hectic lifestyles. He can be reached at:

P.O. Box 1777
Ranchos de Taos, NM 87557
phone: 505-751-1492

Contributors

Some of the stories in this book were taken from books we have read. These sources are acknowledged in the Permissions section. Other stories and poems were contributed by friends of ours in the business world. If you would like to contact them for information on their books, tapes and seminars, you can reach them at the addresses and phone numbers provided below.

A number of stories were also contributed by readers such as yourself responding to our request for stories. We have included information about them as well.

Joan Wester Anderson is a bestselling author and is recognized around the world as an authority on angelic and miraculous intervention in everyday life. Over 2 million copies of her books have been sold. She can be reached at P.O. Box 1694, Arlington Heights, IL 60006.

Robert R. Ball is the executive director of the California Self-Esteem Task Force. He is a nationally known speaker and author, with books on communication and self-esteem. Bob speaks to corporations, schools, associations, and on cruise ships. You can contact him at 572 Schooner Ln., Longboat Key, FL 34228.

Francie Baltazar-Schwartz is a content-based professional speaker who motivates audiences to action. Francie specializes in communication strategies, leadership/coaching and team-building. Francie can be reached on the Internet at http://www.spectracomm.com or by calling 214-373-8075.

Neil Balter is the author of "A Captive Audience," which is excerpted from his book *The Closet Entrepreneur* (published by Career Press). The book is available at bookstores nationwide or can be ordered by calling 800-955-7373 or writing to Career Press, 3 Tice Rd., Franklin Lakes, NJ 07417.

Christine Barnes is a human resources/organization development professional who has worked in Canada and the United States. Currently she works in San Francisco for a large technology company and is seeking others to network with about spirituality in business and leadership. She can be reached at 415-382-8552.

Angela Barnett works for a health insurance company in Minneapolis, MN. She has enjoyed storytelling in many forms over the years. *Chicken Soup for the Soul at Work* provides the perfect opportunity to share her special true story.

Richard Barrett, a member of the Values Team in the Department of Institutional Change and Strategy at The World Bank, is an internationally recognized speaker and workshop leader who specializes in personal and corporate transformation. He is founder of The World Bank's Spiritual Unfoldment Society and author of the highly acclaimed *A Guide to Liberating Your Soul.* He can be reached at P.O. Box 19926, Alexandria, VA 22320 or by calling 703-768-9558.

Ken H. Blanchard is chairman of Blanchard Training and Development, a full-service management consulting and training company. He is the author of numerous books, including the all-time bestseller *The One Minute Manager.* A sought-after speaker and business consultant, he can be reached at Blanchard Training and Development, 125 State Pl., Escondido, CA 92029 or by calling 800-728-6000.

Sharon Borjesson is a former second-grade schoolteacher. She married a Marine officer and became a mother of two, traveling and living throughout our great country. She settled in San Diego in 1969 and started a career in real estate.

Helice Bridges is the creator of the world famous "Who I Am Makes A Difference" blue ribbon ceremony. Her message has reached over 4.5 million people throughout the world. She is a renowned speaker/entertainer, author and master storyteller. Helice specializes in teaching people how to bring out the best in everyone in one minute or less. To order Blue Ribbons or to contact Helice, write P.O. Box 2115, Del Mar, CA 92014 or call 619-634-1851; fax 619-634-2746.

William T. Brooks is a former college football coach and speaks 150 times yearly. His eight books and hundreds of other training tools are used by thousands of organizations. He can be reached at The Brooks Group, 1903 Ashwood Ct., Suite C, Greensboro, NC 27455 or by calling 800-633-7762.

Joyce Ayer Brown is director of Volunteer Services at a nursing facility. She has worked in long-term care for 18 years. She writes inspirational poetry and often reads it for church programs or for the nursing home residents. Joyce can be contacted at her home at 307 W. Elizabeth Dr., Raymore, MO 64083 or by calling 816-331-1233.

Darrell J. Burnett, Ph.D., is a clinical and sports psychologist, parent, national lecturer, author, consultant and volunteer youth league coach. He has been in private practice in Southern California for over 20 years, working with troubled youth and their families and specializing in positive parenting. His publications include *The Art of Being a Successful Youth League Manager-Coach* and *Youth, Sports, and Self Esteem: A Guide for Parents,* and many more. You can contact Dr. Burnett at Funagain Press, P.O. Box 7223, Laguna Niguel, CA 92607 or by calling 800-493-5943; fax 714-495-8204.

Dave Carpenter has been a professional cartoonist since 1976. His work has appeared in numerous publications, including the *Wall Street Journal, Good Housekeeping, Forbes, Better Homes and Gardens* and the *Saturday Evening Post.* He can be reached at P.O. Box 520, Emmetsburg, IA 50536 or by calling 712-852-3725.

Chris Cavert is a nationally known presenter/trainer of Experiential Play and Games for pro-social development. He has written the full-spectrum E.A.G.E.R. Curriculum, used to train child-care professionals. Chris can be reached through the Experiential Specialists, P.O. Box 50191, Denton, TX 76206.

Michael Cody, a retired brigadier general, is an internationally recognized speaker, educator and entertainer. Mike specializes in leadership, motivation, management, communications and historical seminars. He can be reached at 1716 Singletary NE, Albuquerque, NM 87112 or by calling 505-293-3729.

Charles A. Coonradt is the author of *The Game of Work* and *Managing the Obvious*. Both books are referred to as management must-reads. His company, The Game of Work, Inc., has been improving productivity and profitability for its clients since 1973. He is recognized internationally as an author, speaker and consultant. Over 1 million people have heard his unique concepts. He can be reached at 1912 Sidewinder Dr., Suite 201, Park City, UT 84060 or by calling 800-438-6074.

Sandra Crowe is a seminar leader, speaker and coach who presents on topics such as "Dealing with Difficult People" and "Stress Management." She is the author of the tape series *Snakes, Apes & Bees: A Guide to Dealing with Difficult People* and the book *Since Strangling Isn't an Option . . . 12 Illuminating Ways to Deal with Difficult People*. She can be reached at Pivotal Point, 10836 Antigus Terr. #202, Rockville, MD 20852 or by calling 301-984-7818.

Joy Curci has been called the Forrest Gump of the home cleaning industry. She has spent nearly 20 years carrying around keys that unlock the doors to her clients' homes and private lives. Many of these stories are included in her upcoming book, *Spring Cleaning for Your Soul*. She is an entertaining and motivational speaker and still owns one of the largest home cleaning companies in the Northeast. She can be reached at 156 Seas Dr., Jamestown, RI 02835 or by calling 401-423-3732.

Kenneth O. Davis, M.D., is a family physician, addictionologist and nationally recognized speaker on self-care and the patient-physician partnership, which he explores in his upcoming book, *Dancing with Your Doctor*. For a copy of the "Health Yourself" newsletter, call 409-756-3321.

Mary Ann Dockins is a certified/registered master practitioner of NLP time-line therapy and hypnosis. She specializes in the areas of self-esteem, personal power and motivation. She also sponsors workshops for cancer survivors. Mary Ann has been in public speaking for several years and has been a guest speaker on local TV and radio. Contact Mary Ann at 2840 Laramie, Irving, TX 75062, or call 214-256-1312.

Nicholas Economou is the designer of the "Time On My Side" planner and seminar. He has trained thousands of people on personal organization and effective goal-setting. His clients include many of the Fortune 500 companies.

He can be reached at RPO 50009, #15-1594 Fairfield Rd., Victoria, BC, Canada V8S 1G0 or by calling 604-744-1296.

Wyverne Flatt speaks, consults and conducts seminars from Boston to Puerto Rico to Honolulu. He believes that learning and growing are natural and fun. He can be reached at 11107 Wurzbach Rd., Suite 103, San Antonio, TX. Telephone 210-691-2264, fax 210-691-0011.

Celeste Fremon is an award-winning journalist and author of *Father Greg and the Homeboys* (Hyperion), a four-year account of gang life in East Los Angeles. She is a regular contributor to *Los Angeles Times Magazine* and various national publications.

Margaret J. Giannini, M.D., is the former Deputy Assistant Chief Medical Director for Rehabilitation and Prosthetics at the Department of Veterans' Affairs in Washington, D.C. In 1979, President Jimmy Carter appointed Dr. Giannini as the first Director of the National Institute of Disability and Rehabilitation Research. She has published extensively and lectured nationally and internationally.

Barbara Glanz is an internationally known author, speaker and consultant who specializes in creative communication, building customer loyalty and regenerating the spirit in the workplace. She is the author of *The Creative Communicator, Building Customer Loyalty* and *CARE Packages for the Workplace— Dozens of Little Things You Can Do to Regenerate Spirit at Work.* Barbara can be reached at 4047 Howard Ave., Western Springs, IL 60558. Telephone 708-246-8594, fax 708-246-5123.

Randy Glasbergen is one of America's most widely and frequently published freelance cartoonists with more than 20,000 cartoons and several books published worldwide. You can find him on the Internet at http://www. norwich.net/~randy/toon.html.

Rick Halvorsen is a 34-year-old corrections officer from Michigan. He dedicates his story to his father and mother and his wife, Kim, who has stood by his side through good and bad times. Kim was his strength during the war and his inspiration to write "For the Love of My Father."

Jeff Hoye and his company, Strategic Intent, serve organizations such as Ford, Allied Signal and Blue Cross/Blue Shield, and specialize in the hands-on role of the senior executive in large-scale, team-based change. He can be reached at 303-415-2531.

Gary Hruska is assistant vice president of publishing operations at GTE Directories world headquarters in Dallas/Fort Worth, Texas, where he directs and coordinates activities of the Core Business Systems. As a supporter of the processes that won the company the Malcolm Baldrige National Quality Award in 1994, Gary is chairperson of the corporate committee that oversees quality-related activities. He holds a bachelor of science degree from Northern Illinois University in DeKalb, IL, and a master's degree from DePaul University in Chicago, IL.

Susan Jeffers, Ph.D., is the bestselling author of *Feel the Fear and Do It Anyway, End the Struggle and Dance with Life, Dare to Connect, Opening Our Hearts to Men, The Journey from Lost to Found, Thoughts of Power and Love* plus her *Fear-Less Series* of affirmation books and tapes *(Inner Talk for Peace of Mind, Inner Talk for a Confident Day,* and *Inner Talk for a Love that Works).* Dr. Jeffers is a popular workshop leader and public speaker and has been a guest on many national radio and television shows.

Gina Maria Jerome is an author, speaker and publisher. Her specialty is showing businesses how to expand their customer base without the hassle and expense of advertising. Contact her at Over the Wire, jerome@overwire.com, or write 13492 Research Blvd., Ste. 120-126, Austin, TX 78750 or call 512-257-1892.

Martin L. Johnson has spent more than 17 years in the telecommunications industry with Northwestern Bell, Pioneer Hi-Bred, Intl., and AT&T. He is currently a consultant with Comsys Data Services. He holds a B.A. in philosophy from Iowa State University and an M.B.A. from Drake University.

James Kennedy is the president of Success Seekers International and an accomplished entertainer. As a participant in a wide range of sports activities, James has excelled at basketball, which he played for Team Canada, and has been a member of the European professional league. He works internationally with organizations in customer service, total quality, leadership and team-building. Contact James at 519-944-7554.

Marilyn Johnson Kondwani is a speaker/businesswoman whose self-esteem, leadership and aromatherapy workshops inspire people to reach their full potential. A coauthor of *Chicken Soup for the Souls of Black Folks,* and founder of Treasure of Egypt Natural Products, Marilyn can be reached at P.O. Box 1923, Fairfield, IA 52556 or by calling 515-472-1802.

Lapis is a magazine that offers the finest in holistic thinking on the many critical issues in modern life. From spiritual and esoteric insights to political and ecological analysis, *Lapis* presents fresh ideas from many of the world's leading creative figures. Each edition contains striking photo essays, poetry and travel stories. Contact *Lapis* at 212-334-0210.

John Lumsden has transformed New Zealand's meteorological service into a successful weather information business by leading people to enthusiastically pursue a shared vision of the company's future. He can be reached at lumsden@met.co.nz or by calling 011-644-475-9404.

Nancy Noel Marra has been a teacher for the past 16 years. She has a master's degree in education and is a frequent presenter at professional conferences. Nancy was awarded the 1996 Presidential Award for Excellence in Science and Mathematics Teaching. She enjoys writing and is working toward listing the word "author" as part of her personal portfolio. Nancy can be reached at 224 30th Ave. NE, Great Falls, MT 59404.

Hanoch McCarty, Ed.D., is a highly sought-after motivational speakers whose corporate training programs focus on strategies that build employee and customer loyalty as well as freeing creativity and maximizing personal productivity. His work uses the bottom-line power of kindness and integrity. He can be reached at Learning Resources, P.O. Box 66, Galt, CA 95632; e-mail him at kindness@softcom.net or call 209-745-2212.

Dennis J. McCauley has been practicing therapeutic healing bodywork since 1975. He is known for his ability to create a calm, caring atmosphere where people can regenerate, heal and grow as their balance and harmony are restored. Dennis is also a tai chi instructor. He can be reached at 450 Sherwood Dr., #308, Sausalito, CA 94965 or by calling 415-331-8880.

Jeff McMullen is a speaker, entertainer and author with an international reputation for meeting and exceeding the needs of his clients. Jeff speaks on motivation, humor, customer service, change and effective leadership. Contact Jeffrey at 414-954-9300, or at 3315 N. Racine St., Appleton, WI 54911.

Rachel Dyer Montross is employed as a Southwest Airlines customer service agent at Los Angeles International Airport. She is currently studying for a degree in exercise physiology and sports psychology, and is studying to become a certified personal trainer.

Bob Moore is a master speaker and workshop leader on how to build strong character traits and personal motivation in students and employees. He is a noted author and can be reached at 19-B Senate Plaza, Columbia, SC 29201 or by calling 803-799-0493.

Sharon Drew Morgen has changed the sales paradigm with her book *Sales on the Line,* which promotes buyer-focused, service-based sales. She trains companies seeking to bring ethics into sales. She can be reached at 505-776-2509.

John and Ann Murphy became humor therapists after each survived a heart attack. They speak to businesses, associations and individuals from all walks of life who are under stress. Their message is: (S)he who laughs last—lasts! They can be reached at 4 Camelot Dr., Hingham, MA 02043.

Valerie Oberle has been a cast member at Disney World in Orlando, Florida for over 25 years. Valerie is responsible for professional development programs offered to business professionals. For more information, call 407-824-4855.

Sally K. O'Brien, president of S.K. O'Brien, is a speaker, consultant, author, educator and trainer specializing in communication skills. She has been giving professional speeches, workshops and seminars in the areas of presentation skills, sales training and principles of self-esteem for the past 10 years. Contact Sally at P.O. Box 6522, Hilo, HI 96720 or fax her at 808-959-2344.

Jeffrey Patnaude, one of the pioneers in bringing together the worlds of work and spirit, is a master teacher, speaker, author, consultant and priest. A creative and dynamic presence who evokes personal and organizational transformation, he leads 12 associates in serving corporations worldwide in the areas of leadership, management and communication. Write The Patnaude Group, 600 Colorado Ave., Palo Alto, CA 94306 or by calling 800-275-5382.

Rick Phillips is an internationally recognized speaker focusing on highly customized sales and customer-service systems. The author of over 100 articles, Rick speaks to thousands each year on developing an Unfair Advantage. You can contact Phillips Sales and Staff Development at 800-525-PSSD (7773).

Kate Porter is a partner of Demosoft Enterprises, a software/Internet company that specializes in education.

Richard Porter is president and CEO of Service Track Enterprises, Inc., a firm that specializes in high-performance customer service.

Nido Qubein, C.S.P., C.P.A.E., is past president of the National Speakers Association and is an outstanding speaker on sales, management and marketing. His many books include *Get the Best from Yourself, Communicate Like a Pro* and *Professional Selling Techniques.* He can be reached at Creative Services, Inc., P.O. Box 6008, High Point, NC 27262 or by calling 919-889-3010.

Marty Raphael has been sharing her insights into consciousness throughout her 20 years as a corporate executive. Author of *Spiritual Vampires: The Use and Misuse of Spiritual Power,* she may be contacted through her publisher, The Message Co., 4 Camino Azul, Santa Fe, NM 87505 or by calling 505-474-0998.

Naomi Rhode, R.D.H., C.S.P., C.P.A.E., is the past president of the National Speakers Association and is known for inspirational, dynamic speaking to both health care and corporate audiences. She is co-owner and vice president of SmartPractice™, a marketing and manufacturing company that provides products and services to the health care industry worldwide. Naomi is the author of two inspirational gift books, *The Gift of a Family—A Legacy of Love* and *More Beautiful Than Diamonds—The Gift of Friendship.*

John Scherer is the author of *Work and the Human Spirit* and the video-based *Breakthrough Series.* He is also creator of Leadership Development Intensive, a program for expanding the mind, stretching the body and deepening the spirit of the next generation of leaders. Contact The Center for Work and the Human Spirit, 421 West Riverside Ave., Spokane, WA 99201 or by calling 509-838-8167.

Harley Schwadron is a freelance cartoonist whose work appears regularly in *Wall Street Journal, Harvard Business Review, National Law Journal, Washington Post, Des Moines Register* and many other publications. He can be reached at P.O. Box 1347, Ann Arbor, MI 48106 or by calling 313-426-8433.

Michael Shandler, Ed.D., is president of Vision Action Associates, an Amherst, Massachusetts-based consulting firm specializing in organization and leadership development. Dr. Shandler is an internationally recognized speaker and the author of seven books. His most recent book, *VROOM! Turbo Charged Team Building,* has been described by Kenneth Blanchard as a breakthrough book. Dr. Shandler can be reached at 47 Summer St., Amherst, MA 01002 or by calling 413-459-1670.

Kenneth L. Shipley is a designer/writer who specializes in ideas and words for print marketing materials. His work has been recognized with over 50 awards from regional, national and international organizations. He can be reached at 15965 York Rd., Cleveland, OH 44133 or by calling 216-582-4183.

Joanna Slan is an award-winning international speaker and trainer. The author of two books and coauthor of five, Joanna specializes in gender issues, customer service and balance. You can contact her at 7 Ailanthus Ct., Chesterfield, MO 63005 or by calling 800-356-2220; e-mail joannaslan@aol.com.

Jeff Slutsky is an internationally renowned keynoter on marketing without money. His six books include *StreetSmart Tele-Selling* and *How to Get Clients*, and he is featured on a PBS series. You can contact Street-Fighter Marketing in Columbus, OH, at 614-337-7474.

Linda Stafford, author of *Crying Wind* and *My Searching Heart,* is writing a series of romance novels. She lives in Hawaii with her four children, where life is practically perfect.

LaVonn Steiner, M.S., is a motivating international speaker/consultant, and a certified manager and author of 34 performance seminars. Her genius is coaching performance: executive, one-on-one and group. She influences people's attitude and motivates change. You can contact LaVonn at EXCEL Corp., at 701-255-1919.

Mike Stewart, C.S.P., specializes in helping sales organizations overcome sales call reluctance and increase prospecting and closing activity. He speaks internationally and conducts workshops and seminars on consultative sales management topics. You can reach Mike in Atlanta, GA, at 770-512-0022.

G. Stillwagon, D.C., Ph.C., is an author, lecturer, researcher, inventor and technique developer. The chiropractic profession recognizes him internationally for contributions in research in the Derma Therm-O-Graph and Visi-Therm Infrared Electronic Thermography. Patient progress can be monitored and documented visually with these non-invasive outcome measurements. You can reach Dr. Stillwagon at Stillwagon Seminars, Inc., 767 Dry Run Rd., Monongahela, PA 15063. Telephone 412-258-6553, fax 412-258-5611.

Judy Tatelbaum, recognized authority on grief, author of *The Courage to Grieve* and *You Don't Have to Suffer,* is an inspiring speaker/trainer, encouraging people to achieve fulfilling lives. You can reach Judy at P.O. Box 601, Carmel Valley, CA 93924 or by calling 408-659-2270.

Mike Teeley is a professional speaker/consultant. His workshops on customer service and change management have earned him national recognition. His organization is Service Advocate, and he has recently published *Change and the Challenge of Leadership: A Handbook for Organizational Excellence.* He can be contacted at Service Advocate, 3 Butch Songin Circle, S. Walpole, MA 02071; call/fax 508-668-1759.

Art Turock speaks internationally on change, leadership and empowerment. Art's ideas have been featured in *Success* magazine, *USA Today* and *The One-Minute Manager* series. Conducting over 200 interviews per year, he dynamically delivers customized up-to-the-minute material. Art can be reached in Seattle at 206-827-5238.

Glenn Van Ekeren is a dynamic speaker in the areas of personal, professional and organizational development. He is a practicing human resource professional, bestselling author of *The Speaker's Sourcebook*, *The Speaker's Sourcebook II*, and the revisor of *Braude's Treasury of Wit and Humor* as well as *The Complete Speaker's & Toastmaster's Library*. Glenn also pens the popular Potential newsletter. He can be reached at People Building Institute, 330 Village Circle, Sheldon, IA 51201 or by calling 712-324-4873.

Denis Waitley is a well-known author and lecturer. He can be reached at 800-WAITLEY.

Anne Walton is a warm, motivating, inspiring consultant/facilitator/presenter who specializes in change and transition. Anne released her first guided meditation tape, *Enhancing the Journey*, earlier this year. You can contact her at #902-1433 Beach Ave., Vancouver, BC, V6G 1Y3, Canada or by calling 604-682-1626.

Dr. Ann E. Weeks is a nationally known speaker who gives her audiences many everyday strategies for dealing with life's passages. Ann specializes in humor and real-life stories to make her presentations a treat. She can be reached at P.O. Box 5093, Louisville, KY 40205 or by calling 502-458-2461.

Mike Wickett is widely sought-after as a speaker, seminar leader and sales trainer for companies large and small, including IBM, McDonald's, Boise Cascade, Transamerica, Aetna, State Farm, Century 21 and Northwestern Mutual Life. He is president of Mike Wickett Enterprises, his public speaking and business consulting firm.

Steven B. Wiley is a highly acclaimed speaker/entertainer whose audiences include the finest organizations in the world. His exceptional marketing, leadership and interpersonal skills have been lauded by major publications including *Venture, Entrepreneur, Inc.* and *USA Today*. Steve's specialties include sales, leadership, wellness and motivation. He can be reached at 717-359-8733 or at The Wiley Group, 1790 Hoffman Home Rd., Littlestown, PA 17340.

Jonathan Wygant is president of Consciousness Unlimited, providing world-class consultants, keynote speakers and trainers to corporations interested in transforming the workplace into a heart-centered arena. His company provides experts in the following areas: communication, leadership, innovation, productivity, integrity and wellness. Contact Consciousness Unlimited, 3079 Calle Pinon, Santa Barbara, CA 93105 or call 805-569-0654; fax 805-569-9826; e-mail: resource@consciousu.com.

Mohammad Yunus is the founder and director of Grameen Bank in Bangladesh.

The Reverend Aaron Zerah is an interfaith minister, spiritual entrepreneur and author of *From Heaven to Earth: Spiritual Living in a Market-Oriented World*. Known globally as a speaker, columnist and teacher, he serves as director of the Interfaith Seminary. You can reach him at 917 Windsor, Santa Cruz, CA 95062 or by calling 408-459-9484.

GIVE A BOOST TO YOUR CAREER WITH HCI's BUSINESS TITLES

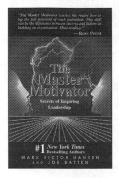

The Master Motivator
Secrets of Inspiring Leadership
Mark Victor Hansen and Joe Batten

Here is *the* definitive book on motivating others from two of the world's most renowned and respected motivational speakers. Joe Batten, mentor to Ross Perot and author of *Tough-Minded Management*, and Mark Victor Hansen, motivator/communicator extraordinaire and coauthor of the bestselling *Chicken Soup for the Soul* series, show you how to achieve top performance from yourself and those you lead: how you can become *The Master Motivator*.
Code 3553 trade paperback **$9.95**

Putting Your Talent to Work
Identifying, Cultivating and Marketing Your Natural Talents
Lucia Capacchione, Ph.D., and Peggy Van Pelt, Ph.D.

We all have unique talents that define who we are to the world. If you haven't yet discovered your unique abilities and put them into action, this book is for you. You'll learn how to identify the innate gifts that make you special. Techniques and case studies offer you a blueprint for developing your talents. You'll also find plenty of no-nonsense advice on marketing your skills for gainful—and meaningful—employment.
Code 4061 trade paperback **$12.95**

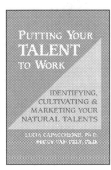

Networking Success
How to Turn Business & Financial Relationships into Fun & Profit
Anne Boe

Networking is the business tool of the 1990s—a must for keeping the competitive edge that separates the successful from the unsuccessful. Here master networker Anne Boe describes ideas for developing, nurturing and growing your relationships, financial contacts and career networks for peak performance on and off the job.
Code 3650 trade paperback **$12.95**

Available at your favorite bookstore or call **1-800-441-5569** for Visa or MasterCard orders. Prices do not include shipping and handling. Your response code is **CWRK**.

Share the Magic of Chicken Soup

Chicken Soup for the Soul™
101 Stories to Open the Heart
and Rekindle the Spirit

The #1 *New York Times* bestseller and ABBY award-winning inspirational book that has touched the lives of millions. Whether you buy it for yourself or as a gift to others, you're sure to enrich the lives of everyone around you with this affordable treasure.

Code 262X trade paperback $12.95
Code 2913 hardcover $24.00
Code 3812 large print $16.95

A 2nd Helping of Chicken Soup for the Soul™
101 More Stories to Open the Heart and Rekindle the Spirit

This rare sequel accomplishes the impossible— it is as tasty as the original, and still fat-free. If you enjoyed the first *Chicken Soup for the Soul*, be warned: it was merely the first course in an uplifting grand buffet. These stories will leave you satisfied and full of self-esteem, love and compassion.

Code 3316 trade paperback $12.95
Code 3324 hardcover $24.00
Code 3820 large print $16.95

A 3rd Serving of Chicken Soup for the Soul™
101 More Stories to Open the Heart
and Rekindle the Spirit

The latest addition to the *Chicken Soup for the Soul* series is guaranteed to put a smile in your heart. Learn through others the important lessons of love, parenting, forgiveness, hope and perseverance. This tasty literary stew will stay with you long after you've put the book down.

Code 3790 trade paperback $12.95
Code 3804 hardcover. $24.00
Code 4002 large print $16.95

Available at your favorite bookstore or call **1-800-441-5569** for Visa or MasterCard orders. Prices do not include shipping and handling. Your response code is **CWRK**.

Extra Helpings of Chicken Soup

Chicken Soup for the Surviving Soul
101 Stories of Courage and Inspiration from
Those Who Have Survived Cancer

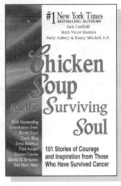

For years, the uplifting stories in the *Chicken
Soup for the Soul* series have empowered individuals who have serious illnesses. Now Jack Canfield
and Mark Victor Hansen have joined with Patty
Aubery and Nancy Mitchell for a special batch of
Chicken Soup devoted to stories of people beating
cancer and finding renewed meaning in their lives.

Code 4029 trade paperback $12.95
Code 4037 hardcover $24.00

Chicken Soup for the Soul™ Cookbook
101 Stories with Recipes from the Heart

Here authors Jack Canfield and Mark Victor
Hansen have teamed up with award-winning
cookbook author Diana von Welanetz Wentworth
and dished up a delightful collection of stories
accompanied by mouthwatering recipes.

Code 3545 trade paperback $16.95
Code 3634 hardcover $29.95

Sopa de pollo para el alma
(Spanish Language Version)
Relatos que conmueven el corazón y ponen
fuego en el espíritu

The national bestseller and 1995 ABBY Award
winner *Chicken Soup for the Soul* is now available
in a lovingly prepared Spanish language edition.
The stories found in *Sopa de pollo para el alma*
are as rich as mole sauce and as robust and invig-
orating as café Cubano.

Code 3537 trade paperback $12.95

Available at your favorite bookstore or call **1-800-441-5569** for Visa
or MasterCard orders. Prices do not include shipping and handling.
Your response code is **CWRK**.

Enjoy a Fresh Batch of
Chicken Soup for the Soul™

Chicken Soup for the Woman's Soul
101 Stories to Open the Hearts and Rekindle the Spirits of Women
Jack Canfield, Mark Victor Hansen, Jennifer Read Hawthorne and Marci Shimoff

As you read *Chicken Soup for the Woman's Soul*, the inspiring stories will nourish you with the strength and beauty shown by women of all ages and all cultures. This delightful book will light up the spirits of women everywhere—from the career woman to the stay-at-home mom; from mothers to grandmothers; from the young woman just starting out to the woman of the world.

Code 4150 trade paperback $12.95
Code 4290 hardcover $24.00

Chicken Soup for the Soul™ at Work
101 Stories of Courage, Compassion & Creativity in the Workplace
Jack Canfield, Mark Victor Hansen, Maida Rogerson, Martin Rutte and Tim Clauss

This volume of the best-loved series features stories of exceptional courage, compassion and dedication in the workplace. Whether you are just entering the work force, well established in a career or retired after years of service, you will find encouragement and inspiration in these stories.

Code 424X trade paperback $12.95
Code 4304 hardcover $24.00

A Cup of Chicken Soup for the Soul™
Jack Canfield, Mark Victor Hansen and Barry Spilchuk

With this collection of brand-new stories—none more than two pages long—you can now enjoy fresh *Chicken Soup for the Soul* whenever you have a few spare moments. Take it with you wherever you go for a quick pick-me-up.

Code 4215 trade paperback $8.95

Condensed Chicken Soup for the Soul™
Jack Canfield, Mark Victor Hansen and Patty Hansen

Canfield, Hansen and Hansen have concentrated their favorite short stories from the *Chicken Soup for the Soul* series in this delectable little volume. The best of the best, now available in one easy-to-carry volume.

Code 4142 trade paperback $8.95

Available at your favorite bookstore or call **1-800-441-5569** for Visa or MasterCard orders. Prices do not include shipping and handling. Your response code is **CWRK**.

Hear the Heartwarming Goodness of Chicken Soup for the Soul™ on Audio

Health Communications, Inc. proudly presents its audio collection of the *Chicken Soup for the Soul* series. Each book is available on tape or CD for your convenience. Brighten your life by listening to these words of inspiration.

The Best of the Original Chicken Soup for the Soul™ Audio
Code 3723 one 90-minute cassette $9.95
Code 4339 one 70-minute CD $11.95

The Best of A 2nd Helping of Chicken Soup for the Soul™ Audio
Code 3766 two 90-minute cassettes $14.95
Code 4347 one 70-minute CD $11.95

The Best of A 3rd Serving of Chicken Soup for the Soul™ Audio
Code 4045 one 90-minute cassette $9.95
Code 4355 one 70-minute CD $11.95

Chicken Soup for the Women's Soul Audio
Code 4401 one 90-minute cassette $9.95
Code 441X one 70-minute CD $11.95

Chicken Soup for the Soul™ Audio Gift Set
Code 3103 6 cassettes, 7 hours $29.95

Chicken Soup for the Soul™ at Work Audio
Code 4428 one 90-minute cassette $9.95
Code 4436 one 70-minute CD $11.95

Available at your favorite bookstore or call **1-800-441-5569** for Visa or MasterCard orders. Prices do not include shipping and handling. Your response code is **CWRK**.

HCI's Guides to Personal Success

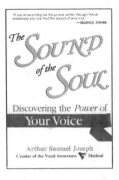

The Sound of the Soul
Discovering the Power of Your Voice
Arthur Samuel Joseph

Voice is your identity; it represents you to the world. Having a confident, commanding voice and persona can make the difference between being heard and being ignored. In this fascinating book, Arthur Samuel Joseph—vocal consultant to stars of the stage and screen, singers, corporate executives, politicians, broadcasters and athletes—shows you how to master your voice, enhance your Self and change your life. You will discover how to develop power through self-awareness and integrate it into total mind/body/spirit wellness.
Code 407X trade paperback **$10.95**

Going Public
A Practical Guide to Developing Personal Charisma
Hal Milton

Risk-taking is key to achieving success in many areas of life, from business ventures to personal relationships. Yet often we fail to reach our goals because fear paralyzes us. This inspiring book is a step-by-step guide to overcoming the fear of any type of performance, developing authentic communication and increasing self-expression. After reading this book, you'll soar to new heights on the wings of renewed strength and creativity.
Code 360X trade paperback **$9.95**

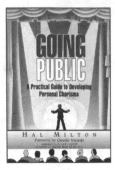

The Art of the Fresh Start
How to Make and Keep Your New Year's Resolutions for a Lifetime
Glenna Salsbury

In *Chicken Soup for the Soul*, Glenna Salsbury told of miraculously seeing her dreams become reality. Now she shares with you her practical, step-by-step approach for tapping into your core being to achieve permanent, repeatable and ongoing self-renewal. This unique approach to goal-setting will teach you to live a life filled with hope, joy and a multitude of fresh starts.
Code 3642 trade paperback **$9.95**

Available at your favorite bookstore or call **1-800-441-5569** for Visa or MasterCard orders. Prices do not include shipping and handling. Your response code is **CWRK**.